KU-415-058

CONTENTS

PREFACE

Anyone who rides a bike is lucky in my book. But I have been especially lucky to be the guy on the bike who was in the right place at the right time. For most of my journalistic career, cycling and my love of it have been things quite separate from writing and my love of that. So, to be given the opportunity that I have – since 2005, a weekly platform to publish on any aspect of the world of the bicycle that catches my eye – has been a privilege as heaven-sent as it was unlooked-for.

Before the Berliner relaunch of the Guardian, in September 2005, I was more used to finding editors rolling their eyes, stifling yawns and remembering urgent phone calls to be made, if they saw me approaching with an idea for a cycling-related piece. I would certainly never have had the temerity to suggest a regular cycling column.

Credit for that goes to the then editor of G2, Ian Katz. This may have come about for no more scientific or solidly researched reason than that, one sunny day, he trundled down the hill past Sadlers' Wells to work and found there were no spaces left in the bike park. Something about cycling was happening out there in the world, so, we asked ourselves, why were we giving a whole spread to cars, yet nothing to Guardianistas' transport *mode de choix*, bikes?

I realise this looks, not for the first time, as if a national newspaper is edited on the principle of "what the world looks like today from Islington". But editors are as good as their hunches, and this one has been borne out. Within a few months, it was clear that the Guardian's cycling column had a decent following – and was flattered by the Independent adding a similar slot to its motoring section.

The early Two Wheels were very short – writing to length was often the greatest challenge. Eventually – "by popular demand" would be overstating it, but thank you to those people who wrote in to ask why cycling didn't get more space – we colonised another of the car review's columns. And despite the eternal fear of the rookie columnist of drying up after a fortnight, there never seemed a shortage of things to write about, and I'm indebted to colleagues, many cyclists themselves, who always had questions and thoughts for me.

Indebted, too, to the hundreds of readers who have written in, over the past two years, with questions, comments, ideas and feedback. Even when critical (usually justifiably), these have almost always gone out of their way to add that they welcome the fact that a national newspaper has given space to a cycling column.

That support only lends force to the sense we all have that the bicycle is truly an idea whose time has come (again). For those of us who care about cycling and its future, it feels as though we are riding the crest of a wave. An unhappy metaphor for a cyclist, I know, but that is what cyclists are saying to one another – and we're just glad to be along for the ride.

Most of the pieces in this collection are Two Wheels columns, but I have also taken the opportunity to republish an assortment of occasional comment pieces, features, interviews and book reviews from the Guardian, some of them predating Two Wheels. I have also added a few essays written for my friends at the cycle clothing outfitter Rapha, for their website (www.rapha.cc), and for the gorgeous quarterly magazine they publish, Rouleur, because I felt they complemented the columns and was glad to have the opportunity afforded me by Guardian Books to reprint them here. I am very grateful to Simon Mottram and Luke Scheybeler of Rapha, and Guy Andrews, editor of Rouleur, for the privilege and opportunity to write for their media, and for their kind permission to reproduce those articles.

I owe also a great debt of gratitude to Ian Katz, for entrusting me with his idea and coaching me to hit the right note at the beginning. And to Katharine Viner, present editor of G2, for her enthusiasm and encouragement, and for giving Two Wheels a new home in the Ethical Living section, when the natural instinct of editors (usually rightly) is to kill inherited columns. Thanks also to the patient and excellent subeditors of G2 – Rick Williams, Julie Reid, Andrew Clarke, Dick Bates and others who have handled my copy, gently improved it, and saved me from making a few howlers. I am very grateful to Lisa Darnell, publisher of Guardian Books, Helen Brooks, its managing editor, and Amelia Hodsdon, the book's copy editor, for all their careful work on this book; and for believing in it in the first place.

My thanks also for the excellent press work of Steve Taylor at Transport for London and Yannick Read at the Cyclists' Touring Club, among many others. An honourable mention must be made of Keith Bingham, of Cycling Weekly, for being more of a mentor in the field of cycling comment than he knows. A special mention also for Brian Palmer, editor of Islay's finest cycling website, thewashingmachinepost.net, who has provided welcome and witty feedback on the column practically every week. A big thank you, too, to all my friends in cycling, who have contributed in small but significant ways to what I know and write about cycling: Philip Burnett, Simon O'Hagan, Graham Bence, Guy Andrews, Dominique Gabellini, Graeme Fife, Grant Young and all the guys at Condor Cycles, Therese Bjorn at Velorution, Jack Thurston of Resonance FM's Bike Show, John Mullineau of londoncyclesport.com, and scores of others from the weird and wonderful world of the bikie. And a general thanks, finally, to all the readers who have corresponded either directly with me or with the "bike doctor".

Last but not least, I would like to express my deep gratitude to my family: my parents, Geoff and Caroline Seaton, for always showing an interest; my daughter, Lola, and son, Joe, for putting up with my cycling obsession and only grumbling moderately when dragged along to bike races (essential research!); and to my wife, Anna Shapiro, who has not only borne this bike thing with, on the whole, heroic patience and good humour, but who has also been a generous reader and, where necessary, a fine critic.

Matt Seaton
May 2007

ONE

ON THE CAMPAIGN TRAIL: CONTRA THE FLOW

The public image of cycling has improved enormously in recent years. A pastime that was marginal and eccentric has become cool and hip; a mode of transport that was dowdy and down-at-heel has become glamorous and chic. Still, cyclists themselves are not much liked. For many, we are a nuisance: rude, impatient, selfish – and self-righteous with it. There is a grain of truth in that: perhaps it's because we spend a lot of time in the saddle, but we know how to be pains in the arse. But if cyclists are the grit in the oyster, it also means that we have the potential to become the pearl of great price.

What has changed in my adult lifetime is that cycling has moved from the margins of transport policymaking, literally side-lined as road users, to the mainstream. As sustainability and tackling congestion by getting people out of their single-occupancy cars have moved to the top of metropolitan political agendas, cycling has become part of the solution. Gradually, it is becoming axiomatic in town planning that cycling has to be a substantial element in the mix of transport modes.

For cyclists, of course, this is simply common sense writ large – with some transport policy jargon and wonkery thrown in, for reasons of professional etiquette. Everyone who rides a bike for practical purposes does so because they have discovered that nothing beats it for speed, reliability, convenience and pleasure. What is perceived by the unconverted or uninitiated as smugness or self-righteousness is, for cyclists, simply the consciousness that riding a bike is just so obviously and absolutely the right thing to do. And that absolute conviction can, perhaps, make us zealous on occasion.

Yet, we are a minority and a physically vulnerable one on the road, so we have to speak out loudly to make ourselves heard. Cycling needs its campaigners and advocates, partly because the field of transport is already dominated by extremely powerful institutional and commercial interests (think of the size of road-building budgets, the power of motor manufacturing and oil industry lobbies, the popular enthusiasm for driving), and partly because the way traffic is managed on our roads has the automatic effect of placing different groups of road user in competition with each other (for resources and rights, and for plain physical space). Most cyclists I know therefore have a consciousness of themselves "as a class". And just as you cannot get on a bike and ride on a public road without being confronted by these issues, so also you cannot write about cycling and fail to engage with them.

Thursday January 25, 2007

So often people tell me the reason they don't cycle is because they don't feel safe. As a result, I generally feel it's my duty to set them right. To point out that cycling is not, in fact, dangerous (by the standard statistical measure, it's safer than walking). To put the case that the health benefits of the exercise far outweigh any risk. And to advise that, if you get some training, you can give yourself confidence and make yourself safer on the road.

Most of the time, I convince myself as I write. To admit otherwise feels taboo: it's letting cycling down. For the same reason, I don't even like to think about the dangers myself – let alone write about them. Mostly, my defence is that I am such a competent cyclist that I minimise risk. But there is an awkward voice in my head that now and again asks the question I have no answer to: what if a really careless driver doesn't see you and hits you from behind, just mows you down? What then?

What then, indeed. This was the scenario 10 days ago when a car ran into the back of a group from the Birkenhead North End Cycling Club, out on a Sunday training run. Mel Vasey, 53, a local bike shop owner, was killed; another rider badly injured. The young driver was said to have been dazzled by low sunlight. This was just a few miles from where, a year earlier, three members of the Rhyl Cycling Club were killed when their group was hit by a car whose driver had lost control on black ice. (He was later found to have three defective tyres, although the police, in their wisdom, ruled this out as a factor.) And in a few days' time, a Norfolk man is due to be sentenced for causing the death by dangerous driving of Zak Carr, one of the country's top time triallists, in 2005. Carr was struck while riding on the hard shoulder of the carriageway by a car whose driver was so dazed by lack of sleep that he failed even to stop immediately after hitting Carr.

The common theme here is that, yes, sometimes there are "accidents" (incident is surely the word we should always use, given the prevailing force of human error in such cases), about which we cyclists can do nothing. The unpalatable truth, however far I go out of my way to avoid it, is that cyclists are vulnerable road users. And cars are lethal objects.

Harsher penalties are all very well, but will they touch those males aged between 17 and 40 who drive fastest and, quite wrongly, consider themselves infallible? How do you turn around that cultural leviathan of complacent recklessness that does not even realise how cheaply it holds others' lives until called to account, after the fact and too late? Another question I don't have an answer for.

Thursday March 1, 2007

When I'm in the bit of my head that is cyclist (rather north of 99%, if you ask my wife or children), there are not many things I find to agree with motorists about – even though I am a driver, too, albeit as infrequently as possible. But on the undesirability of speed bumps, I could perhaps make common cause.

I'm not sure which I dislike more: the traditional "sleeping policeman" type that runs right across the road, or the "stepping stone" sort, which seems even more pointless, as most cars are wide enough to travel over them comfortably at 30mph if the driver aims for the middle of each.

In theory, the speed bump should be the cyclist's friend, as the object is to slow down, or "calm", vehicular traffic. But in practice, cars aren't calmed at all by speed bumps – almost the reverse, as they brake for each bump and then accelerate in between, burning more fuel and increasing their emissions, carbon and otherwise. Possibly the one useful effect they do have is to create a disincentive for drivers to use residential roads as rat runs, but as congestion increases, that benefit is ever diminishing. If it's between getting in the hump in a traffic jam, or riding the humps but getting somewhere ... well, which would you choose?

But these could be drivers' own objections, and motorists even favour speed cameras over humps, with a large majority also approving 20mph limits in residential areas. So why would a cyclist mind them – apart from the fact they don't really achieve what they're meant to, and are arguably counterproductive, that is? Well, cars at least have suspensions. Unless you're riding a mountain bike (and they aren't good in an urban environment), a cyclist's suspension is his or her bottom. All right, making people ride their bikes over speed bumps is not likely to make it into the CIA interrogation techniques handbook any time soon, but it's not pleasant either. At anything more than a creeping pace, you get sufficient jolt to have to momentarily "unweight" your body in the saddle as you hit the upside, and then again on the downside. And I do mean downside: speed bumps are, literally, a pain in the arse.

But what about the stepping-stone type, you ask: you should be able to ride through the gaps, perineum unperturbed. You would think so, yes, but almost invariably, parked cars make passing on the inside of the bump either hazardous or downright impossible, so then you have to swing out into the middle of the road to pass through the outer gap – and that is not always safe or advisable either. So, more often than not, you're obliged to go straight over the infernal thing. Odds on that it'll be one of those really evil, straight-edged, angular ones, which can only have been thought up by a modernist architect *manqué*, taking out his disappointment at being a mere road engineer on the poor cyclist.

Unloved, unfit for the purpose ... what is the point of speed bumps?

Thursday March 22, 2007

Here is a startling fact to get your attention: between 1999 and 2004 (the period for which figures are available), 85% of female cyclist fatalities in London involved a heavy goods vehicle. To put this into context, the number of cyclists killed in the capital has been fairly constant for several years, running at about 20 a year – this figure on streets where, Monday to Friday, about half a million people take to their bikes every day. That perspective is necessary, because this is not a story about how dangerous cycling is. It is a story about the particular problem cyclists have with HGVs, and what we can do about it.

But the 85% figure is shocking – and, sadly, reinforces the anecdotal evidence: in the past week, two young female cyclists have been killed on London's roads in incidents involving lorries (Amelia Zollner, 24, and Madeline Wright, 26). There is a gender differential here that, in effect, makes HGVs a feminist issue. The disproportionate casualty rate for women, discovered here in an unpublished report from the London Road Safety Unit, confirms the finding of an earlier 1990s survey published in the British Medical Journal: while HGVs are a major threat to men, male cyclists are more likely to die in a car-related incident; women are more than four times more likely to be the victim of an HGV collision.

So, why are women so much more at risk? Without more research, we can only speculate. But one answer may be that men are more aggressive in their riding style, and this means they are less likely to get trapped on the inside of an HGV – in slow-moving traffic, they either get through the gap quickly, or will pass it on the outside.

The numbers above all come from London, but there is no reason to assume that what makes HGVs dangerous to cyclists, and to female riders in particular, does not also apply elsewhere in the country, especially in built-up areas. The classic scenario involves the left-turning lorry, whose driver has not seen the cyclist on the inside, with the result that the rider is crushed against barriers or dragged under the rear wheels. I have lost one friend (Charlie Curthoys, 39) this way, and almost lost another – only by good luck did the driver hear her screams as she went down, and stop.

What is the solution to this carnage? According to Cynthia Barlow, a retired scientist from London University, whose daughter was killed by a left-turning lorry in 2000 and who now campaigns for the road safety organisation RoadPeace (www.roadpeace.org), the haulage industry could be doing much more. Drivers need training and education, lorries need modern mirrors to eliminate blind spots and other design features such as additional indicators, side-bars and sensors. And firms need to accept a degree of corporate responsibility by treating the death of a member of the public involving their goods vehicle as a work-related fatality, rather than washing their hands as if it hasn't happened actually on their premises.

Ultimately, though, we have to look after ourselves. We can also get some education: Transport for London is putting an extra £1m into cycle training next year, and the Cyclists' Touring Club has a phone service to locate an instructor near you (0870 607 0415). But I have my own simple rule: unless I can see it is 100% safe to pass, I never get on the inside of an HGV. Just don't go there.

Wednesday September 27, 2006

News editors seem to have a thing for cycling stories these days. You can hardly open a newspaper without seeing some item or other. It's usually knocking copy – making out either that cycling is dangerous, or that cyclists are (surely some contradiction?) – but harmless enough. But there is one bike-related story I never want to read again: the one that ran last week about a suicide bomber in Afghanistan who rode into a crowd and detonated himself, killing four Canadian soldiers and wounding dozens of Afghans, including at least two children. The Taliban has claimed responsibility.

It's not the first time a bicycle has been used this way. The Tamil Tigers have done so, as have Palestinian militants and Iraqi insurgents. Apart from the horror at such carnage, when a bicycle is named as the suicide bomber's mode of transport, I am filled with a particular melancholy. It is almost as if I feel guilt by association; I hate to think that so pure an idea could be tainted by such desperate cruelty.

Which is odd of me. Car bombings are far more common – and destructive – yet do motorists flinch inwardly at hearing of one? I doubt it, and there's no rational reason why they should.

For cyclists, though, there is one rational reason why we should fear a link being drawn between suicide bombing and bicycles. It has long been the policy of the Metropolitan police not to permit bikes to be parked in the vicinity of the Houses of Parliament, dating from the time when the security threat came not from jihadists but from Irish republicans.

This was absurd. Michael Collins may have ridden a bike between ambushes of British troops during the war of independence (1919-21), but when the IRA wanted to attack the British establishment in the 1970s and 80s, it didn't bother with bicycles: it was car bombs and lorries loaded with mortars. The police impounding bikes around Whitehall always seemed to me more a snobbish concern with street hygiene than with any terrorist threat.

Yet the bogey of the bike-as-bomb lives on. The excuse given by Arsenal FC for failing to provide adequate bike parking at its new Emirates stadium in north London is precisely this: that the police advise that al-Qaida might send in ranks of bicycle-riding suicide bombers. Not that one wants to contemplate it, but if the threat is that serious, then presumably the police will be excluding all motor traffic and frisking every fan going in. No, of course, they won't. There is parking for 500 season-ticket holders' cars beneath the ground. It is clearly considered beyond al-Qaida's capability to acquire a season ticket.

Arsenal has committed itself to a travel plan that has 88% of matchgoers arriving by means other than private car. Despite that target, here we have a major public building fighting its planning obligations to provide suitable bike parking. As a precedent, that strikes me as far more dangerous than the phantom bike bomber.

Wednesday December 14, 2005

Extensive polling I have conducted on behalf of this column (that is, at least three conversations at Christmas parties) reveals an interesting and widespread belief about the very visible increase of cycle use in the capital. Namely, that the growing number of Londoners taking to their bikes is due neither to local authorities putting in cycle lanes, nor to Transport for London's five-year plan, nor even to the congestion charge – but to the terror attacks of 7/7.

It's a cracking story partly because it says yah boo sucks to the terrorists. But it also appeals to our perversity and contrariness. This is a tale about how what decades of earnest campaigning and publicly funded urging failed to accomplish (getting people back on bicycles) happened overnight. We love it because it hovers somewhere between the law of unintended consequences, the proverbial ill-wind never blowing anyone any good, and our primal desire for a redemptive theme. But is it true?

What did happen is that a lot of new bikes were sold after 7/7. Even allowing for chains such as Halfords puffing up its figures, there is plenty of evidence of a boom in the bike trade. But did those extra purchases translate into greater use? Well, a significant number of people did find a new way to work: passenger numbers on the underground were down 15-20% after the attacks. But, because of line closures, the tube's capacity was down by a similar amount. And bus use actually went up – despite the Tavistock Square bus bomb.

And bike use? Dramatic numbers such as an extra 50,000 cycle journeys a week made convenient handles for journalists and were still being reported many weeks after the bombings. What, in fact, occurred was a spike in the graph that lasted a fortnight (up, on average, by 15%, or 4,000 trips a day); then it was back to normal.

But "normal" here means a steady upward trend. "What the bombings did for bike use" was a wonderful good-news story, but what's really getting results is pro-cycling policy and increased spending. Isn't that actually the best news?

Wednesday October 26, 2005

For the past 11 years, on the last Friday of the month, cyclists numbering from a few score to, sometimes, several hundred have gathered near Waterloo bridge in London at 6pm. When some kind of quorum is achieved, they ride around en masse for a couple of hours before dispersing. There is no planned route, no identifiable leader, and no explicit political aim.

Critical Mass, as this "unorganised coincidence" is known, is organised enough to have a website – but only to insist that it is not a protest; more a fun ride to "assert our identity as cyclists". If you're interested, there is probably a Critical Mass near you; many UK cities have one. I've only joined the London ride once. There was an exhilarating carnival spirit, but after an hour or so, I felt I'd got the idea and pedalled off.

Until now, the ride has enjoyed benign policing designed to minimise its impact on other traffic. But last month, officers – on bikes – handed out leaflets explaining that, in future, if the Metropolitan police was not informed in advance about the ride, then it would be deemed an "unlawful demonstration" and participants "liable to arrest". This Friday will be the first test of the "get tough" stance, but it has already drawn criticism, notably from the mayor's road safety ambassador. In an open letter to Sir Ian Blair, Jenny Jones criticises such "heavy-handed application" of the Serious Organised Crime and Police Act (2005). According to the Met's public order branch, she says, Critical Mass does not meet the criteria for a political demonstration.

What could have inspired such folly? Sadly, the Met seems to be copying the NYPD's crackdown on Critical Mass, which began in August 2004 when the Republican national convention came to New York. Around 237 cyclists were arrested. Across the bridge, Brooklyn Critical Mass continues, but in

Manhattan, a ritualistic game of cat and mouse between cops and massers has taken place ever since – a costly lesson in how little can be achieved by pointlessly macho policing.

Zero tolerance: the most overrated concept of our age.

Wednesday September 21, 2005

If you ride a bike, you probably find this. The non-cyclists of my acquaintance – and there are a few; I'm not prejudiced – often take me to task for some cyclist's misdemeanour they have witnessed. (Obviously I become responsible for the behaviour of cyclists everywhere, at all times.)

The biggest bugbear of non-cyclists is cyclists who run red lights. Riding on pavements comes a close second, probably followed by not using lights at night.

On the red-light-running charge, I'm afraid it's bang to rights. Do cyclists think that the rules of the road do not apply to them? Do they believe that some Harry Potteresque invisibility cloak masks them as they sail blithely through a pedestrian crossing on red?

Call me conformist, call me square, but there is not a lot of room for ambiguity here. Post-Saussurean linguistics may be perfectly correct in asserting that the link between signifier and signified is entirely arbitrary but, some wit once pointed out, even the most ardent deconstructionist still stops at red as if it meant something.

The problem with disobeying traffic signals is that it is anti-social – and ultimately self-defeating. Crashing reds is a menace to some road users (eg pedestrians), and a wind-up for others (eg motorists). But above all, it costs all cyclists public goodwill, for the sake of a handful of seconds. We're talking about a kind of moral short-termism, where the choice is between the negligible inconvenience of stopping, and making people feel completely justified in hating you.

So challenge the behaviour, you say. Yeah, right. Have you ever noticed how defensive British people are? Offer even the mildest correction and we go on the effing counter-attack. Perhaps especially with cyclists, because we like to think we are intrinsically better than the people in petrol-burning metal boxes, any reproach tends to get an instant nuclear response.

But worst of all is the person whom red-light-runners turn you, the law-abiding cyclist, into: an ugly combination of censorious, yet cowardly and cynical. It's enough to make you see red.

Wednesday December 21, 2005

"You know what drives me mad? Cyclists who go through red lights ..." If you are a cyclist, it's not a matter of if, or even when, you will have this conversation. It's how many times a day. Even cyclists are obsessed with the red light debate, filling letters pages in cycling magazines and web chatrooms with ferocious arguments and counterarguments.

As a card-carrying bikie, I can't get to the canteen and back, or across a room at a party, without being buttonholed on the subject. After my daughter's school Christmas show, a parent came up and said she and others were going to start a campaign of protest because four children had been knocked down by cyclists running reds nearby in recent weeks. Being a cyclist herself, she was also thinking of badges or T-shirts bearing a slogan such as "I stop at red", because she knows the problem is not just that it's dangerous to pedestrians but that it seriously pisses off other road users.

And because there's nothing more visible than a cyclist breezing through a red light, it is spectacularly bad PR. According to an official at Cycling England, the body charged with promoting cycle use, one of the chief reasons why the Department for Transport is so unenthusiastic about cycling is because the Home Office dumps on its doorstep the vast postbag of letters about the outrages perpetrated by "Lycra louts" – cycling without lights, riding on the pavement, and, above all, ignoring traffic signals. In other words, when a cyclist runs a red light, the rest of us might as well get out the old revolver and fire one off at our collective foot.

So what is to be done? More enforcement would be one solution. In the City of London, bicycle-mounted officers have been handing out penalties to miscreant cyclists. But most forces have few officers equipped to do so and unofficially admit that they can't enforce the Highway Code where cyclists are concerned because, in practice, they can't catch those who flout the law.

Another partial answer is training. Cycling England recently gave £1m to the Cyclists' Touring Club (UK cycling's biggest voluntary organisation) to establish a network of more than 1,000 accredited cycling trainers. Transport for London pays for cycle training for Year 6 children in primary school – with the result that many 10-year-olds in the capital are a good deal better at hand signals than adults. But training is designed to give those who don't yet cycle on the public highway the skills they need to start. It won't reach those who, frankly, could do with a spot of "re-education".

That leaves only one plausible option: cyclists should be licensed. We should have to pass a test in which we demonstrate proficiency and knowledge of the rules of the road. Cycling organisations would say that the last thing the cause of cycling needs is another barrier in the path of potential riders. Cyclists themselves will ask why they should have to pass a test when, unlike cars, bicycles almost never cause serious injury to others. But most people would pass without difficulty and with a very useful reminder of traffic etiquette. It would be a formality little more arduous than getting your car taxed or renewing your passport, and quite a lot more fun.

Cyclists rightly want more measures and facilities in their favour, but as these rights are granted, it is time to accept some responsibility. Pedestrians and other road users deserve considerate, safe cyclists. Because civil servants so long made cyclists second-class citizens by planning roads that in effect designed us out of the system, we have acquired a tremendous sense of self-righteous entitlement – even to behave badly. It's really time we got over it. Taking a test would show we have.

Wednesday April 26, 2006

We're in the middle of Bike to School Week (what do you mean, you didn't know?). And Bike Week, and Bike to Work Week, are on the horizon. Initiatives like this are completely admirable; I have nothing but praise and gratitude for the people who make them happen and put on events to promote bike use.

And yet ... I find something about them depressing. I think it's to do with a sneaking feeling of impotence and pointlessness. So much effort and good intention go into these things, but do they really make a difference? Do they, finally, get more people cycling – in this case, kids to school? I hope they do, and believe me I hate myself for being so negative (and that's depressing, too).

My kids, who are both 10, do sometimes cycle to school. They did every day when I took them myself; they didn't have a choice, after all. But now they are old enough to walk to school by themselves or with a friend, that's how they prefer to go: on foot. It's still healthy and better than travelling by car, but I'm trying to get over the slight feeling of rejection and wasted effort at having failed to inculcate the bike habit.

When I asked my daughter why she prefers walking (even though her school is far enough away to make cycling quite a bit quicker), she said it's because she prefers leaving school with her friends rather than going round the back and wrestling with a bike lock on her own. Nationally, only 2% of kids cycle to school. The percentage might be higher at my daughter's inner-London school where there is a certain proportion of bike-oriented, *bien-pensant* parents like me, but my daughter is still voting with her feet: not enough of her peer group cycle, and she doesn't want to be a freak like her father. Hard to argue with that.

My son is less concerned about the social cost of cycling, but he has to ride mostly on the pavement, which makes getting to school an obstacle course. On the way back, there's a bus lane he can use, which he feels safe in. But on the way there, it's a main road – a dual carriageway, with no bus lane. Any car that sticks to the 30mph limit gets overtaken on the inside by the majority of drivers, who see it as a half-mile drag strip. I'm not wild about cycling up this road myself.

And that's what gets me down. These noble people could make every week of the year a Bike to School Week and still make almost no impression on the number of kids riding their bikes. What we really need are more bike lanes, bus lanes, and strictly enforced 20mph zones within two miles of every school. Until then, what sane parent is going to let their child cycle to school?

Wednesday February 1, 2006

You might be forgiven for thinking that smuts went out with steam engines, but they're still with us. You need only cycle through traffic for a few minutes to find the evidence right under your nose. Or rather, right on it.

Ride to work, take a tissue and wipe your face with it – you should find tiny streaks of soot. Small, but perceptible. And that's just the stuff we can see. The urban atmosphere has a lot of undesirable additives – sulphur dioxide, nitrogen oxides, carbon monoxide and ozone for starters. All more or less irritant or toxic, and virtually all produced by motor vehicles.

The phasing-out of leaded petrol has taken one substance out of circulation only to replace it with another: benzene, a known carcinogen. But vehicle exhausts produce many other organic compounds, known as polycyclic aromatic hydrocarbons. Aromatic, perhaps, but hardly fragrant: many PAHs, too, have been linked with cancer.

We encounter PAHs in smoke of all sorts, and smoke is made up of masses of microscopic particles – in the academic jargon, PM10s (particles measuring less than 10 microns in diameter, a micron being a millionth of a metre). These minuscule specks of soot are so small they can penetrate deep into our lungs. And, whereas our pulmonary system is pretty good at expelling unwanted but inert matter such as dust via mucus, the PM10s produced by diesel combustion are sticky. These tarry little lumps laced with PAHs adhere deep inside our lungs for an indefinite stay.

There was little sentimentality among cyclists, therefore, over the killing-off of the old Routemaster buses. With their anti-quated, smoke-spewing engines, they've been killing us off for years. Good riddance! Research has suggested that the air breathed by motorists is worse than that breathed by cyclists, but the latest information from Imperial College London contradicts this. According to a recent paper, cyclists are exposed to double the level of particulate matter (80,000 particles a cubic centimetre) that motorists are ($40,000pt/cm^3$), and more than pedestrians (50,000). Worse off still are bus passengers, with people travelling by taxi breathing the dirtiest air of all (both around 100,000). None of this is good news, but even a cloud of smoke has a silver lining. The local pollution caused by a passing smoker was off the scale: even standing behind a bus is better than passive smoking.

At least smoking in public is on the way out, unlike the diesel engine. The Clean Air Act, which abolished the dreaded pea-soupers caused by coal fires, is 50 years old this year. Given what we know about modern forms of pollution, a new round of tougher emissions standards really would be a breath of fresh air.

Wednesday March 29, 2006

Changing all the clocks may be a drag, but I am extra-grateful for the arrival of British summer time. If I leave work in time, I can get home without bike lights.

What a liberation. The worst thing about cycling through the winter is not the cold, nor the wet, but all the clobber you have to schlep: the lock, the waterproofs, the gloves ... and the bike lights. They're always switching themselves on at the bottom of my bag, blinking away in the dark so that the batteries are flat when I need them. I keep several corner shops in business with my demand for Duracell AAAs.

So I will be glad to dispense with lights for a few months. And not only my bike bag, but also my conscience will be lighter: it means I can cycle without breaking the law – because my bike lights, though excellently fit for purpose, do not conform to British standards and are therefore not legal.

But if they were, I would still be riding in breach of regs, as my bike does not have reflective amber strips on the pedals. That's right: the law says even grown-ups have to have them. Unless you do, you too are a felonious bike-rider.

Despite consultative papers from the Department for Transport, and yards of advice from assorted interest groups, somehow the muddle continues over statutory recognition for the now-ubiquitous flashing LED light. In short, you would have to be using a pair of those huge, clunking, paleolithic Ever Ready lamps – the ones that took two DD batteries, each weighing about a pound – to be sure of being legal. If you could get them to work. My memory is that they would conk out and refuse to work if you so much as went over a bump.

But does it really matter if you use the modern "illegal" lights, as long as you are lit up? Day to day, it seems not. Provided you display a reasonable level of "conspicuity", as the jargon has it, then the police turn a blind eye; only those riding without lights are ever likely to get a ticket. The only hitch might be if you were knocked off by a car and ended up in court, where the motorist's smart-arse lawyer would argue that your failure to use lights and reflectors complying with BS6102/3 constituted "contributory negligence".

Laughable perhaps, but this is a phrase we could be hearing

much more if a proposed change to the Highway Code goes through. A seemingly innocuous piece of rewording now implies that cyclists must use cycle routes and cycle lanes if available; not to do so – by choosing to stay on the main road, for instance – could be construed as contributory negligence. Having spotted the danger CTC is leading a campaign against this nonsense, which you can sign up to online (www.ctc.org.uk).

It seems a good idea to support it – with conspicuity.

Thursday May 10, 2007

At the weekend, I was among the many cyclists who rode up the road that leads to the Roehampton gate of Richmond Park, in London. This stretch is about three-quarters of a mile long and dead straight, so it's easy for cars to pass provided there's nothing coming the other way. For about half that distance, there is a bike path marked on the pavement on one side of the road. In order to use it, therefore, a southbound cyclist (like me) would have to cross the lane of oncoming traffic, and then, after about half a mile, re-cross the road to join the carriageway when the lane runs out. Along the way, the bike path is interrupted several times by driveways and side-streets. No rational cyclist would ever choose to use it.

But that didn't prevent the 4x4 driver (aren't stereotypes comforting sometimes?), whose progress of speeding at 35mph was possibly impeded by having to drive at a law-abiding 25mph for about 20 seconds, shouting out of his side-window that I should get in the bike lane and off the road. I suspect we have all been there.

It's such a common occurrence, it's utterly trivial. Or would be if we did not still face the threat of a revised Highway Code, due out this year, which is so worded to allow the legal interpretation that cyclists might be guilty of "contributory negligence" if they fail to use available cycle facilities. The old Highway Code text suggested simply that cyclists "use cycle routes when practicable". No problem there. The new code advises us to "use cycle routes and cycle facilities ... wherever possible."

Suppose, then, that Mr 4x4 Driver makes a hash of passing me and causes a collision. The new Highway Code could enable his lawyer to claim that I had a liability by failing to use the "cycle facility provided". You would think courts would not be so daft as to accept this argument, but never underestimate the asininity of the law: last year, Daniel Cadden had to appeal against a judgment of "inconsiderate cycling" in a case brought by police who had decided he should have been using an inconvenient bike path rather than the road. In January, with the backing of the cyclists' defence fund (www.cyclistsdefence-fund.org.uk), he won a retrial and was acquitted.

CTC – the UK's national cyclists' organisation (www.ctc. org.uk) – is ever alert to the issue and, with its encouragement, 11,000 cyclists have written to their MPs over the past year. There is also a Downing Street website petition (http://petitions.pm. gov.uk/roads4 bikes) you can sign.

Last year, when asked in parliament about the new Highway Code forcing cyclists off the road by its legal implications, the then transport minister Derek Twigg replied that: "The simple answer is that it will not." Why do I not find this response wholly reassuring? Perhaps because of the considerable latitude for Sir Humphrey-esque obfuscation opened up by what might be the "complex answer". Yes, minister?

Wednesday May 31, 2006

You must have seen the advert. It's everywhere at the moment – it fills billboards twice on my short trip to work. This is the Ford ad for a new car called the S-MAX. Which looks like some kind of people carrier, but it's hard to tell because the photo of the four-wheeled vehicle is dwarfed by a picture of a powerful-looking cyclist in a skinsuit riding a virtual bike whose wheels are, in fact, Ford-branded alloys.

The slogan is "S-MAX your life", while a strap elaborates: "The new Ford S-MAX. Feel the difference." It strikes me as interesting that a major motor manufacturer is using the image of a cyclist to market its car. At one level, I've no objection if a company wants to devote several million pounds to making cycling look sporty, sexy and glamorous. As an index of changing attitudes, it does suggest an encouraging shift in the image of cycling.

But the old-fashioned lefty bit of me, the cynic on my shoulder, is muttering darkly about exploitation and hypocrisy. There is something perverse, after all, about using bikes to sell cars.

Ford is a company that likes to boast about its green credentials – using renewable energy technologies at its plants and recyclable materials in its manufacturing. And it makes much of its "citizen responsibility", with a community football initiative aimed at disadvantaged youngsters.

But how green and responsible is this, from its own recruitment literature? "One of our most popular perks is the Privilege Car Scheme which means that you can purchase up to three Ford cars (plus one Volvo, Jaguar or Land Rover) at a discounted rate every nine months." A new car every three months: that's really going to save the planet. But as Ford seems so keen on cycling's healthy, athletic image, I have a few suggestions for improving its public relations.

Instead of discounts on cars, they could offer employees a tax-free bike under the Cycle to Work scheme: a lease-purchase arrangement that enables staff to save as much as 50% on the price of a new bike and accessories. Then they could adopt a travel plan to encourage more people to bike to work. By installing new bike-parking spaces and changing facilities, and offering a cash-for-miles incentive, GlaxoSmithKline – on the other side of London from Ford's Dagenham plant – almost doubled the number of employees it had predicted would cycle to work.

When it comes to sport, the choice is huge. Ford could do anything from sponsoring a racing squad (as Persil used to do), to linking up with local clubs to promote cycle sport at grassroots level. So come on, Ford: S-MAX your corporate responsibility. We'll all feel the difference.

Thursday April 13, 2006

One of my favourite ever bits of graffiti was on the wall of a public library. The building had steps up to the entrance and then, to the side, a wheelchair ramp. But then, beside that, was this short length of iron railing that emerged at an angle from the wall and then zigzagged back into it. Perhaps it was supposed to protect pedestrians from runaway wheelchairs. Or provide a handy outside tethering place for dog-owners who wanted to borrow a book. Who knows? It was a truly baffling piece of street furniture. So the graffiti asked, wonderfully apropos and very simply: "What is this?"

The railings, and the words on the wall, have long gone. Perhaps, finally, the council was embarrassed into answering the question in its own taciturn way by removing both. But the "what is this?" spirit lives on. And nowhere is it more alive than in Warrington.

Warrington is where it's at, especially in cycling circles, because the local cycling campaign there has established something of a cult following for the regular photo feature on its website: "Facility of the Month".

It's a richly sardonic archive of some of the most spectacular cycle-lane nonsenses ever perpetrated by well-meaning but ham-fisted councils. We have lanes that go right through bus stops, beautifully surfaced lanes blocked by telephone boxes, routes that run not for miles but for just a few feet, routes helpfully shoehorned in between parking places mere yards apart, and a whole variety of arbitrary, unscheduled endings with lampposts, bushes, fences and crash barriers.

Go and look – it's worth a few good giggles. Or it would be if some of them weren't downright dangerous, and if the sheer folly of it all didn't make you want to weep with frustration. And there is a serious downside. There are still plenty of councillors up and down the land who bear a grudge about what they see as a case of public money being squandered on an irritating special interest group: that is, cyclists.

It is not difficult to detect their resentment of what they see as politically correct pandering in the contemptuous tokenism of these lanes. You have to ask yourself whose interests are served by installing routes so badly designed and poorly engineered that cyclists go miles to avoid them: what better way to block future funding than to be able to say, "Well, we tried this, but nobody uses them, so what's the point?"

But cyclists are finding a way forward, despite all the deadends and pointless diversions put in their path. To a great extent, what we see courtesy of the Warrington cycle campaign is a hangover from the past. In many areas, the "road to nowhere" bike lane belongs to the bad old days. Heroic biking groups such as Sustrans and CTC have invested masses of time and money in re-educating traffic engineers and helping local authority transport officers establish "best practice" guidelines. Transport for London, championing its own Cycling Centre of Excellence, publishes a fat folder of cycling design standards for every kind of bike facility you can imagine. So there's no excuse any more for installing potential facilities of the month.

The whole philosophy has shifted. The mindset behind many older bike routes is typified by the sort of lane that offers you a route up on the pavement, perhaps at a pinch-point in the road, only to dump you back into the traffic 100 metres later. Clearly, this wasn't for the cyclists' safety or convenience – it was about getting you out of the way of the motorists. But priorities have changed, and the car is king no more.

The problem is that the joke facilities are still with us, like a hangover that won't go, presumably because of a lazy "Oh well, it's better than nothing" view on the part of local authorities.

Actually, no – it's worse than nothing. And here's why: if the proposed new version of the Highway Code becomes statutory, then cyclists who have accidents in the road could find themselves in court being told that their decision to avoid a cycle facility, no matter how badly designed, was "contributory negligence". That's right: from a legal point of view, you would be better riding in the pavement lane that carries you into a hedge than on the public highway next to it. CTC is conducting a vigorous campaign to amend this new wording of the code (and you can sign up at www.ctc.org.uk). One thing we should know by now is that it doesn't pay cyclists to be complacent about the wisdom of our legislators and elected officials. After all, look what we get when they try to do something nice for us.

Wednesday November 9, 2005

Something is definitely up. All my adult life, I have been used to feeling, well, a bit of a freak for going everywhere by bike. Whatever function you arrived at, you were always conscious of being the odd one out: everyone else was better dressed, not conspicuously perspiring and not toting a bulky bag full of waterproofs, mini-pump and bike lights. Those like me have just had to put up with the fact that the rest of the world regarded us as somewhere between harmless eccentrics and foolhardy sociopaths.

But change is afoot: cycling is good news. Last week, there was the record-breaking copper. PC Diederik Coetzee has been striking fear into the criminal classes of Mansfield, in Nottinghamshire, by charging about on a bicycle arresting them all. The average bobby makes fewer than 10 arrests a year; the South African emigre has collared more than 300 suspects already in 2005. Mountain Bike Maurice, our local hero is popularly known as.

Yet the most glaring example of the new trend was when the Tory leadership hopeful David Cameron was widely photographed a couple of weeks ago astride his bicycle. In the past, this would have been political death. Sure, it was OK for Boris Johnson to wobble around town on a bike because his whole image is old-school daffy. But with Cameron it has become a signifier of being just the sort of get-up-and-go, with-it, modern politician the Conservative party needs. As the Observer columnist Andrew Rawnsley noted: "When William Hague tried to advertise his zest by wearing a baseball cap, he was judged to be horribly naff; when Dave Cameron gets himself pictured in a cycling helmet he is treated as the acme of cool."

But it's not just that cycling is no longer uncool; it's much bigger than that. Cycling is the coming thing, and cyclists are the new ruling class. As ever, America is a decade ahead of us: George Bush is a born-again mountain biker (the luckless John Kerry a keen roadie). Bikes rock and bikes rule. I should be over the moon, but somehow I was happier when we were outlaws and weirdos.

Thursday February 1, 2007

People always say that there is a rash of roadworks in the spring not because the roads need repairing after the wear and tear of winter, but because local authority transport departments realise that they have still got a big chunk of change in their budget – which must be spent before the end of the financial year or funding will be cut for the next one. Spreading cynicism around is an antisocial habit, so I will only say that I hope it is not true. And that I hope they won't leave it till March to start work round my way.

It is well and truly pothole season. I don't know how many holes there are in Blackburn, Lancashire, but I bet I could pretty quickly tot up 4,000 in the roads in my borough. In places where they have real winters, entire stretches of asphalt can be deformed, crevassed and cratered by "frost heave", but I have yet to hear of distressed surfaces here being blamed on "the wrong sort of temperature". Instead, it is chiefly rain that seems to do the damage – rain and heavy bus traffic. Most of the time, cyclists gain considerably by sharing bus lanes, but in these winter months the buses give the bit of road we use a proper pounding.

All it takes is one wet day and on the way home holes will have opened up that weren't there in the morning, a debris of gravel strewn across the blacktop like spilt muesli. Only less wholesome, obviously. Potholes are a real menace to cyclists, responsible for everything from buckled wheels to broken teeth, and worse. They have a particularly nasty habit of opening up beside manhole covers, creating vertiginous, sharp-edged ravines ready to swallow bikes whole and spit their riders out well-chewed. Most treacherous of all is the "dark and stormy night" pothole, which lurks cunningly concealed as an innocuous puddle when it is, in fact, a monster of a black lagoon.

Local authorities do have a statutory responsibility to make swift repairs to any surface that might constitute a hazard, and generally they respond with alacrity. Not so surprising when you measure the price of filling a hole against the cost of litigation. Unfortunately, all too often, they effect a temporary repair with a species of asphalt that resembles a black molasses cakemix. It only has to look like rain for this friable material to become so much grit in the gutter again.

The only tactic open to the long-suffering cyclist, who could be excused for wondering whether the US air force had decided to use the route of the No 29 for a spot of carpet-bombing practice, is to report the holes. Cycle campaigns used to provide ready-addressed postcards for the purpose, but times have moved on: CTC has just launched an online service (www.fill thathole.org.uk), which is just peachy to use. Try it and, I promise, you'll soon be going out of your way just to find holes. Here's to more roadworks.

Wednesday January 18, 2006

It ought to be a match made in heaven: bicycles and trains, arguably the two most sustainable forms of transport. All you need to do is ride to the station, buy a ticket, put your bike on the train, relax with a cup of coffee, and then ride off to your destination when you reach the terminus. It's fast, convenient and door-to-door – all boxes ticked. Trains and bikes: a perfect synergy for clean, green travel.

If only. Have you tried going by train with a bike recently? It's a nightmare – hell on wheels, in fact.

Let's say I'm going inter-city. I get to the platform in good time, ready to put my bike in the guard's van: "Hang on, have you got a reservation?" A what? For a bicycle? "You need a reservation for the bike." But I bought my ticket online and it didn't say anything about needing a bike reservation. "That's as may be. You still can't bring that bike on this train without a reservation."

Or let's say I'm travelling on a local service. I check at the ticket office: no reservation required, carriage free of charge. Ah, that's better. "But you can't travel at peak periods." (Southern's Brighton to London line is now the latest to join this trend.) Grrr!

And even if I don't need to travel at rush hour, suburban services on trains with sliding doors generally have no places for bikes. The guard vans of yesteryear, which could carry up to a dozen bikes, have gone along with the old "slam door" rolling stock. Now I have to park my bike awkwardly in the doorway and jump up every five minutes to apologise and move it when the train stops. An excellent example of progress and modernisation making some things much worse.

What's more, post-privatisation, you practically need a research fellowship to discover the intricacies of your local train operator's policy on carrying bicycles. With about 30 companies running services, there is a kaleidoscopic variety of terms and conditions, all subject to alteration at short notice. National

Rail offers a guide – one "made possible by Brompton Cycles", a leading manufacturer of folding bicycles. You can hardly blame Brompton's opportunism, it's not its fault if folding bikes are the only sort train operators are willing to tolerate.

It's enough to make one weep. But is it all bad news? Not completely. Many stations have improved their facilities, putting in more cycle parking. Security can be dubious, however – last time my son locked up his bike at our local station, the saddle was gone when we came back. And I can't help feeling that adding a few extra stands is partly just a low-cost sop to the cycling lobby.

In Germany, for example, they really get the integration thing: trains are designed so that they carry scores of bikes. Apparently, they run on time too.

Tuesday April 12, 2005

Sometimes I almost miss the bad old days. Twenty years ago, 10 even, cyclists in London could style themselves, at least in their own minds, as courageous urban guerrillas: bicycle-bound, bandana-wearing anarchists, who daily braved the hostile chaos of city traffic to get to their destination. There was an implicit camaraderie, because we were an embattled minority, outlaws living on the edge, enjoying a certain dangerous glamour. Even if most motorists just saw us as a nuisance.

Most motorists still see us as a nuisance, but in London they have had to come to terms with our presence. The cycle lanes – once a joke, now much improved – and advance-stop lines at intersections have marked out in graphic fashion that cyclists have a right to road-space. The subliminal message may be more significant than the practical effect: cyclists belong, it says to other road users; they have legitimacy. Traffic calming measures and speed cameras have also helped to make the capital's roads seem a less scary environment.

Sad as it is to say goodbye to the old badass image, I have to admit that conditions for cyclists have improved immeasurably in the capital over the past few years. In part, Mayor Ken Livingstone can take credit for seeing cycling as part of the solution to the city's transport problems. The congestion zone's effect on traffic density in inner London has also proved a boon: cycling is reportedly up 30% in the area. Transport for London's budget for cycling is going up from £7m to £19m to "grow" bike use. As more people take up riding to work, others feel safer on their bikes and join them – it is, in every sense, a virtuous cycle.

As a boost to the 2012 Olympic bid, the mayor has also welcomed back the Tour of Britain professional cycling race to London this year. Last September, I was one of well over a hundred amateur riders who grabbed the opportunity to take part in the supporting race on closed roads around the streets of Westminster. It was fast and furious, with lots of crashes, but it was also fantastic – many spectators said it was more exciting than the pro race. The last time anything comparable had happened was when the Tour de France visited southern England in 1994.

In London, then, the humble bicycle seems – despite all types of obstacles and a kind of instinctive English resistance to anything so continental in style – to have won not only institutional acceptance, but real public prestige. It feels as though cycling has finally reached, to coin a phrase, a critical mass.

Which is great if you live in central London. Elsewhere, however, things are not rolling along quite so sweetly. Having failed to deliver on the rashly ambitious targets for increasing cycle use that it set for itself back in 1997, the Labour government seems to have lost interest almost entirely. The National Cycling Strategy Board has just been replaced by a new quango, Cycling England, but, to the frustration of its own members, it is a cinderella organisation. The NCSB had advised the government that the new body would need a budget of at least £70m (chickenfeed by comparison with road-building costs) to start delivering results; it got £5m – £2m less than Transport for London was spending on cycling before it tripled its expenditure this year. Not exactly a shining example of "the vision thing", especially when government ministers would only have to look out of their windows to see how much has changed in London.

In so many ways – improving public health, making city centres sustainable, reducing car dependency and cutting CO_2 emissions – cycling is the future. London is winning that race, even if much of the rest of the country seems stuck in low gear. Dangerous glamour? Take it from me: it's overrated.

Thursday May 3, 2007

I've had my share of run-ins with drivers. Nothing really ugly, just verbals, but it's astonishing how they colour your day: it's probably quicker to metabolise the unwanted adrenaline than it is to let go of an unresolved argument.

Then I had a sort of Damascene moment. There was a period when I used to go out on rides with a couple of other guys and every time we would have a contretemps with a motorist. It gradually dawned on me that it was not, in fact, that drivers were getting worse on Wednesdays (the day of our regular ride; we were all freelance loafers then). When one of our number started shouting at a driver who had wound down her window to ask directions, I realised something had to give.

Funnily enough, if you don't go around looking for a fight, you generally don't find one. Accepting that it can be best to let inconsequential instances of other road users' stupidity or carelessness slide, rather than automatically getting revved up into confrontation mode, has definitely improved my quality of life.

But this week I have to acknowledge that pacifism only gets you so far on a bike. On my way home, I was riding down a narrow back street when a car coming the other way decided that I should be taught a lesson – just for my temerity at being there, I suppose. Although there was room for us to pass each other safely, he drove directly at me, forcing me to brake sharply at the kerb. Even then, he went by so close that his wing mirror clipped my forearm.

I hadn't fallen. I wasn't hurt. But I was stunned, I think, in the way that people who have been mugged often are – just at the shockingly unprovoked nature of the attack. I rationalise it now as an assault: I was lucky enough not to be hurt, but this man hit me with his car as deliberately as if he had swung a baseball bat at me.

I turned and ran up the road to get his number plate, which I did. He saw me in his mirror, gave me the finger and was gone. I rummaged for my notebook to write down his details, and saw then that the driver behind, who had witnessed the whole incident, had pulled over. He had taken the number, too – what a good citizen. I was so grateful because the next thought that occurs to you in these situations is to ask yourself what you did to deserve it. Blame the victim? Never underestimate the capacity of victims to blame themselves.

I called the police and went to the station. Even as I queued wearily for my turn, and then filled in the form, I could feel my sense of outrage ebbing away. What's the point, said the cynic on my shoulder, nothing will happen. Well, we will have to wait and see.

Thursday March 15, 2007

If you've ever had to wait for a bus, the name JC Decaux will probably be familiar to you. That's because it appears on the bus shelter under the advertising poster. It probably also appears on every hoarding you see from the bus, because JC Decaux is Europe's "number one outdoor advertising company" (and number two in the world).

It's a good business to be in. Its founder, Jean-Claude Decaux, semi-retired at 69, is ranked by Forbes magazine at 154th in its 2006 world's richest list, with a net worth of $4.2bn. Not for nothing does the French newspaper Libération refer to him as "*le roi du mobilier urbain*" – that's "the king of street furniture" to you. And the latest bit of street furniture to catch his eye for its commercial potential is the bicycle.

Two years ago, in his home town of Lyon, JC Decaux teamed up with the city authorities to launch a radical new bike-rental scheme. Dubbing the system Vélo'V (now more catchily rebranded as Cyclocity), JC Decaux was essentially updating earlier efforts at bike pools with improved technology to overcome the problem of theft and ensure a return on investment. Thus, what began with the 60s, anarchist-inspired White Bike Plan in Amsterdam, where bicycles were provided by the city, unlocked and free for public use, was reinvented as an electronic swipe-card subscription service with a less utopian motive.

But if it gets people on bikes, then all well and good. In May 2005, JC Decaux installed 2,000 bikes, deposited at 175 drop-off points in France's second-largest city. Within weeks, 20,000 people had signed up for the scheme, which gives the first half-hour of use free. The number of subscribers has since risen to 60,000. Up to 16,000 rentals occur daily, equivalent to each bike being used by 15 people, who, on average, travel 1.7 miles in 17 minutes. Or a total distance of 25,000 miles every day. A good result, you would think.

On the back of this success, other cities followed Lyon's lead and Vienna, Córdoba, Brussels and now Dublin are pursuing the same track, in partnership with JC Decaux – with London viewing the initiative "with interest", according to Transport for London. Jean-Claude is nothing if not ambitious: he wanted to showcase the bike-rental scheme in Paris. But then Clear Channel, another outdoor advertising company, spoiled his plans with a bid on a grander scale. JC Decaux's response was typically tenacious: halt the original tendering process with an obscure legal challenge, and triple the number of bikes it had first thought of, trumping the American competitor. As Libération sardonically reports, JC Decaux's revised bid would have given Paris a bike park every 200m: overkill, perhaps. Now Clear Channel has launched its own suit, and the whole business is stalled.

What has got slightly lost in all this is whether bike pools really work. Invariably greeted with initial enthusiasm, these schemes often fail down the road: the bikes are heavy and not much fun to ride, and end up being poorly maintained, vandalised or stolen. The risk is that "visionary" local politicians end up footing the bill for an expensive white elephant foisted on them by the operator, while the local bike trade suffers in the meantime from the publicly subsidised competition. So, the question not yet answered is whether it's really true that people are not cycling just because they don't have a bike to hand.

Tuesday September 12, 2006

The eternal paradox of the bicycle seems to be that at the very time it is most popular, it is destined also to be at its most unpopular. When cycling first took off as a craze in the 1890s, periodicals were soon full of editorials decrying the reckless young men (and they were mainly male) who raced around literally frightening the horses. Even today, supposedly, cyclists can be prosecuted in the UK for the antique offence of "furious riding". Sadly, it seems that the more people notice people riding bikes, the more they perceive them as a nuisance. In cycling, what goes around, comes around: once we had "scorchers" (as they were known in the US); now we have "Lycra louts".

The latest proposal to deal with the two-wheeled menace is that all bicycles should be required to have bells, so that riders can warn pedestrians and others of their approach. It is already the case, since 2004, that all new bikes sold must be fitted with bells, but as things stand, there is nothing to stop buyers removing the bell as soon as they leave the shop. But now, it was reported yesterday, the government is considering making it compulsory for all bikes, old and new, to have a bell. According to the Times, the transport minister, Stephen Ladyman, plans to put the issue out for public consultation. If the proposal were to become law, cyclists would face prosecution for riding without a bell and a maximum fine of £2,500.

You might expect the cycling lobby to be up in arms about such a flagrant example of nanny-statism, but it seems to regard it as a not-too-serious piece of policy kite-flying.

"Certainly, no consultation is under way," says Tom Bogdanowicz, the campaigns manager of the London Cycling Campaign. "I don't know if this is something that's a realistic proposal."

"I've no reason to believe it's being taken seriously," comments Roger Geffen, who runs the policy department of CTC – the UK's national cyclists' organisation. "Officials [at the Department of Transport] are denying any action – though they're not ruling it out."

The prospect of police officers issuing spot fines for bell-less-ness seems scarcely more credible than the idea floated by the London mayor, Ken Livingstone, that cyclists might have to display a licence plate so that the red-light runners and pavement riders could be caught on camera. This in a world where only a tiny proportion of motorists committing the demonstrably more dangerous offence of using a handheld mobile phone while driving are ever brought to book.

If I'm honest, though, it's not the enforceability issue that animates my opposition to bells. Actually, it's more gut aversion than reasoned opposition. I wouldn't want a bell on my bike (any of them): on a racer, it would spoil the clean lines and go-fast look; on my town bike, it would be another bit of clutter on the handlebars, along with light brackets and the like.

Let's face it: bells are not cool. They're a bit old-lady-on-a-step-through-frame-with-a-skirt-guard, aren't they? Not to be sexist and boys'-toysy about it, but a bell would do nothing for my image. To put it on a slightly higher plane, cycling to me is an aesthetic practice, as well as just a mode of transport. Ugly and kitsch, bells are simply in bad taste.

I realise this point of view would probably not carry much weight with any civil servant tasked with a public consultation on bicycle bells. So let me add that I would rather slow down and say something reasonably courteous to a pedestrian than use a bell. To me, there's something superior and buttonholing about using a bell – an implicit "Make way" tone in its ring.

Occasionally, I'll whistle a warning when approaching a crossing where it looks as though people might step out unawares. But even that can seem rude. The best way of avoiding conflict with pedestrians, I find, is to avoid them altogether.

"My feeling is that pedestrians like to have a polite verbal warning – it works for me," says Bogdanowicz. "And it encourages interaction, which is what life is all about."

Bogdanowicz's prescription seems closer to the spirit of the Highway Code, which does not stipulate use of a bell, but calls on cyclists to "be considerate of other road users". Both he and Geffen agree that a bell is perfectly good for alerting walkers to your approach if you're riding along a canal towpath or in a park, but when push comes to shove on noisy, urban streets, cyclists are better off using their brakes.

"No one should kid themselves that bells have anything to do with road safety," says Geffen. "What the national standard for cycle training says is that you should have your hands covering the brakes at all times. In an urgent situation, you need your hands and should use your voice."

Geffen suspects that if there is any momentum behind the proposal, it derives from "frustration with errant cyclists". In other words, it comes from a misdirected desire to punish cycling's evildoers, the pavement terrorists: I know, let's humiliate them by making all the bastards fit bells on their bikes! Which is not to say there's not a problem with inconsiderate cyclists, but that compulsory bells are not the practical or rational answer to it. We've been here before, and bells were not the solution then: it all goes in cycles.

Wednesday March 8, 2006

A question for you. How many cyclists would you guess were prosecuted last year for going through red lights? Four thousand ... 400 ... 40? I don't believe in deferred gratification, so I'll tell you: the answer is four. Imagine being one of those four who got collared: given the frequency with which cyclists do run red, you'd be thinking to yourself, "Jeez, what are the odds against that?"

And you have to wonder what kind of flagrant violation the four must have perpetrated to excite the interest of a police officer. Were they also naked and letting off fireworks as they breezed through the traffic signals?

A few weeks ago, I wrote a piece about cyclists and red lights, in which I argued that we cyclists need to put our own house in order: if we want to be treated with respect by other road users, we should start earning it. One way, I said, would be for cyclists to get tested and be licensed. OK, this was silly (please don't write and tell me so again), but I also mentioned a much better initiative. A group of parents at my daughter's primary school were planning a campaign to stop cyclists running a red light near the school, where four children had recently been knocked over – by cyclists. Which gives the lie to the notion that it's a victimless crime.

The school's week of action has just happened, and it was a huge success. It had the support of both the local cycling campaign and the police. Stickers were handed out, homemade placards were waved, the Vauxhall MP Kate Hoey came along, and an ITN news crew covered it. So, for 20 minutes every morning for a week, many of the 60% of cyclists who had been riding through the red light were successfully, if temporarily, re-educated.

But the beauty of this little story is that it doesn't end here. The owner of an independent bike shop in York called Cycle Heaven read about the Lambeth parents (many of whom are cyclists themselves) and realised it was exactly what he'd been wanting to do.

In a matter of weeks, Andy Shrimpton has mustered the support of the Bicycle Association, the Association of Cycle Traders and the sustainable transport charity Sustrans for his nationwide initiative: "Stop at red".

People are encouraged to visit the campaign's website, stopa-tred.org, to sign the online pledge. "If we think we're such good citizens by choosing to cycle (and, dammit, we are), why can't we extend our civicmindedness to our behaviour on the streets?" asks Shrimpton.

Grassroots citizen action: you can't beat it. So wouldn't it be nice if the official membership organisations – the Cyclists' Touring Club, British Cycling and London Cycling Campaign – saw fit to join it?

Wednesday January 11, 2006

It is impossible not to feel haunted this week by the terrible story of the four cyclists killed in North Wales last weekend. Members of Rhyl Cycling Club were out on a Sunday training ride when a car lost control on an icy bend and ploughed into the group. A 14-year-old boy was among the dead.

As well as the local grief caused by the Rhyl CC deaths, this awful news has repercussions far beyond. Thousands of other cyclists will have been out on similar "chain gangs" on Sunday, and this will have sent a shudder through them all. Yes, it is a freak event – but one not unheard of. Last July, in Germany, a car crashed into a squad of Australian racers, killing one, Amy Gillett, and leaving two others in a critical condition. In October, one of Britain's most talented time-triallists, Zak Carr, was hit and died while out training in Norfolk. Everyone in cycle sport either knows of, or knew personally, someone who has been killed on their bike.

And it doesn't take black ice. When I go out early on Sundays, it's common to see cars stuck in hedges and garden walls demolished. I'm just grateful this phenomenon peaks on Saturday night, some hours before I'm on the road.

So will this latest tragedy deter the hardcore of club cyclists? Probably not. We all rely on the calculation that the chances are it won't happen to us. For the more casual cyclists, however, perception of danger is everything. I suspect that those pictures of mangled bikes strewn across the road will be all the disincentive they need.

But just how dangerous is cycling? It is not a simple question to answer. In 2004 (the last year for which figures are available), 134 cyclists were killed on British roads. Terrible, yes, but in relative terms? In fact, you could call 134 deaths a "good month" for motorists – 1,671 car users were killed in 2004. Absolute numbers, though, can be misleading: a better measure is the frequency of casualties occurring. By distance travelled, cars look safer, with 2.7 deaths each billion passenger km (public transport is better still: 0.2 for buses; 0.1 for trains). Cyclists die at a rate of 25 each bn km, but then most do much less mileage than motorists. So although I clock up 5,000 miles a year by bike, which is way more than average, I'd need to live 5,000 years to stand an odds-on chance of dying on my bike.

Presumably cycling is more dangerous than walking? Not so – 671 pedestrians were killed in 2004, at a rate of 43 per billion km. But the trend for all road casualties (except motorcyclists) is downward, especially for cyclists: fewer by a third in the past decade. And the more people cycle, the better other road users adjust, and the safer it is.

The tragedy in North Wales gives us all pause. But if there is one thing the cyclists of Rhyl would not want, it would be for us to stop riding our bikes.

TWO

MEAN STREETS: ADVENTURES IN URBAN CYCLING

For most of us, most of the time, cycling is not an excursion. It is about utility, getting somewhere we need to be, rather than recreation. Which does not mean it can't be a pleasure trip, too. There is a wealth of satisfactions to be gained from riding in town and city. For one, I love the sense of ownership of urban topography that exploring and getting around a city by bike gives me: the knowing and belonging that carrying a mental map affords the urban cyclist.

One of my most vividly remembered moments on a bike would be riding back over the George Washington Bridge and seeing Manhattan island stretched out to my right besides the shimmering expanse of the Hudson river. As if that privileged view of New York wasn't enough, I had also hooked up with a Harlem-based rider who pointed out Mike Tyson's pigeon loft on top of a building in the 120s.

But it's an ambivalent relationship we commuters and city-trippers have with our natural habitat. For every experience of glorious bike-boulevardiering and cyclo-flaneurism, there will be half a dozen scares, slights, near-misses and nasty confrontations. You have to be robust and bold to be comfortable riding in busy traffic, yet also exercise a judicious mix of being assertive and knowing when discretion might be the better part of valour. Even so, there will always be moments of being bummed out. Dark, wet winter evenings will test even the hardiest and most committed cyclist's resolve. But, in my experience, even the grimmest urban bike journey still beats the fug and frustration of the alternatives.

In some respects, life has been getting better for the daily cyclist – although I am very aware that living and riding in inner London, where much has been done to boost cycling and with success, can provide a too-rosy view of the general experience. But I believe we find ourselves at an interesting moment, somewhere between feeling like the oppressed minority we once were and becoming the progressive vanguard of a sustainable future.

Cyclists are by instinct individualists and so have an uneasy relationship with being part of the collective solutions dictated by transport policymakers and town planners. That is a conundrum for the advocates and lobbyists, but it also throws up dilemmas every day, as we respond to the behaviours of others and they react to ours. But that subtle dialectic of city cycling is, to me, what makes the whole experience so inexhaustibly fascinating.

Wednesday October 5, 2005

Most cyclists seem to relish the feeling of belonging to an embattled minority. And what defines "us" is mostly our common disdain for "them" – the assorted sinners of the road-going universe: U-turning black cabbies, oblivious bus drivers, flash gits in sports cars, school-run mums in SUVs, Royal Mail truck drivers "going postal", the ubiquitous white-van man. It's astonishing – and possibly a little outrageous – the number of stereotypes we carry around in our heads.

But imagine the tables turned. What do cyclists look like if we see ourselves as others see us? We may think we are all just individuals united by our choice of personal transport, but I guarantee that, for every cyclist, someone sees a stereotype. "Lycra lout" is the obvious one. We may not wish to own it, but drivers would definitely say they know one when they see one. But not all derogatory tags come from outside. Sports cyclists sometimes talk about "nodders" – referring to the unconscious habit of many casual riders to nod their heads up and down as they pedal. Mean? Absolutely (but just look around).

Others? Well, there is "courier-dude" on a track bike without brakes. And "messenger-wannabe", indistinguishable except for having brakes. Then there's "campaigner-commuter", usually riding a well-travelled touring bike covered in stickers. Behind is "sit-up-and-beggar", pedalling in inappropriate footwear the same bike they had when they were students (basket optional). And not forgetting "mountainbike-macho", the guy (invariably male) who will always overtake you again if you get in front.

It is easy to get offended by such reductive labels. But it's not just blind prejudice; we use them to predict driver behaviour. For example, Q: what is the likelihood of this vehicle ahead of me at the lights turning left without indicating? A: taxi 10%, white van 40%, SUV man talking on his mobile 90%, etc. And I suspect motorists are watching cyclists and doing the maths. Stereotypes? Don't knock 'em. They keep us alive.

Wednesday March 1, 2006

I made a serious mistake this morning. Not fatal, obviously, but the kind of mistake that actually might be injurious to health – someone else's, if not mine.

My error was to draw the attention of a motorist to one he had made: turning right without indicating. I was turning behind him and, seeing his window wound down, said something about his non-signalling. Back came a colourful stream of invective. In the heat of the moment, I could think of no worthwhile reply without resorting to obscenities myself, so all I managed was a feeble: "Nice language, too!" Which only resulted in a further volley of abuse ricocheting off nearby buildings.

After that delightful start to the day, I stalked into the office, furious. What is it with motorists that they react to even a mild criticism of their driving as if you've personally insulted their mothers? An hour later, when my rage had subsided, I went back over the incident. What was it I'd said that had provoked such a ferocious response?

"Thanks for indicating – not!"

OK, so the sarcasm was puerile. Right there, my chances of getting even a grudging acknowledgment, let alone an apology, went from close to zero to rather less. So I had to ask myself what my intervention had achieved. Answer: another driver who would feel utterly homicidal towards cyclists for several hours and fairly hostile for an indefinite period thereafter.

There is a problem with motorists. I know because I am one, and I hate the person I become behind the wheel. Put me in charge of a car and I metamorphose from a sane and rational Dr Jekyll into a rampant Mr Hyde. And it's not just me. Unfortunately, motoring does not create an environment that rewards courtesy and consideration: drive like a competitive jerk and you will get there quicker. I resist it but, sooner or later, I lapse into the general pattern of passive-aggressive mean-spiritedness, grandiosity about one's own skill and power, and casual disregard for just how dangerous a fast-moving tonne of metal really is. The genius of Kenneth Grahame was to realise there is a bit of Mr Toad in us all.

This is not to say that cyclists are any different. There are plenty of people who ride bikes with much the same mentality; it's just that it doesn't usually affect anyone but themselves. And they just get sweaty. Except when they get themselves into slanging matches with motorists. If you go out with the "right" (ie, wrong) attitude, you can have a fight with a driver every time. Again, I've been there and done it.

But, as of today, I'm through with such uncouthness. When a motorist cuts me up on my bike, I'm just going to count to 10 and ride on by. It's my very own traffic karma measure. I'll let you know if it works.

Wednesday September 28, 2005

Is there a feeling worse in the world than coming out of the cinema, theatre or restaurant, going to the railings where you locked up your bike … and finding nothing there?

Having one's bike nicked may seem trivial next to all the death, war, famine and pestilence in the world, but believe me, if it's your bike, then it looms pretty large. A bicycle, after all, is never just a bicycle. A friend and companion, yes, but in a way something more intimate. A bicycle expresses your personality, it becomes both a physical extension and an emotional part of you. Lose your bike and you lose a precious piece of yourself.

As the late Elizabeth Kübler-Ross might have put it, there are three stages of grief in a bike-theft bereavement. First, the heart-in-mouth double-take of bewilderment (shock), swiftly turning through anguished disbelief (denial) to, finally, a sick-to-the-stomach mortification (anger and acceptance).

People who have been burgled often speak of a feeling of violation. To have a bicycle stolen is to experience a similar sense of affront, beyond the merely material loss. What makes a bike theft creepier still is that the thief removes not only the bike but almost always the broken lock too. Obviously, there is a rational explanation for disposing of the criminal evidence, but it has the effect of seeming to deny that there ever was a bike there that belonged to you. That is a peculiar annihilation.

Of course, there are people out there for whom a bike is, in fact, just a bike and no more. For them, I assume, the theft of their bicycle is treated as an inconvenience resulting in the filing of an insurance claim. A replacement bike is then supplied and – because a new bike is by far the most desirable to thieves – very often soon stolen again. Insurance premiums rise, the bike trade profits, and so the world goes.

But how sad and soulless to live without that attachment to your bicycle: better to have loved and lost than never to have loved at all. But best of all to have a nice old bike that no one would bother to nick in the first place.

Wednesday November 30, 2005

And another good thing about cycling: no one I meet is ever stuck for something to say to me. Naturally, I always take the conversational bait – and then find that my ability to notice the glazed expression on the other person's face gets impaired once they've got me started on bikes.

But what I hear all the time from people is that they would ride a bike but don't because they feel it's too dangerous; they're scared of cycling in traffic. I completely sympathise, but, of course, I disagree. I usually find myself about to say: "But look at me: I cycle all over town and I haven't had an accident in 15 years." I stop myself because: (a) it sounds unbearably smug; and (b) even I can see that, tempting-fate-wise, it would be a very stupid remark.

But experience does count for something. You follow certain rules: you try to make eye-contact with drivers; you avoid getting into the blind spot of anything big; you check over your shoulder before pulling out, and so on. It's obvious stuff, but it keeps you alive.

In fact, far from feeling frightened, I love cycling in traffic. It's a superbly absorbing challenge of anticipation, judgment and skill. And it has a social dimension: traffic movement is rich in a non-verbal communication that enables constant, subtle accommodations between road users. If you learn not to treat it as a combat sport, or a zero-sum game where your loss is my gain, then you discover that negotiating the rush hour can become a kind of improv choreography.

At least, that is what I was thinking this morning before I got an email from my oldest cycling buddy – with the news that he'd been knocked off by a car pulling out, without looking, at a mini-roundabout. He dislocated a finger and had some stitches in his head, but was otherwise, thank God, all right.

So now I'm not sure what the moral is. Statistically, cycling is safer each mile than walking (or driving). But I probably shouldn't be kidding anyone, myself included, that bicycling around town is like ballet on wheels.

Thursday May 11, 2006

It's good to know there's still something we Brits are world-class at. Even if it is bike theft. The veteran German cycle tourist Heinz Stücke, who has been travelling the world on two wheels since 1962, had no sooner got off the boat at Portsmouth and pitched his tent than some scally had made off with the bike that had done more than a third of a million miles. The last time Herr Stücke's bike was nicked was a decade ago, in the wild east of Siberia, since when he has established a world record for the most countries visited by bicycle (211).

It is fair to say that his security measures left a little to be desired. "I covered my bicycle with a canvas and tied it up with string and bungee cords outside my tent," he said. "I even left my tent door open so that I could see it, but when I awoke at 3am, it had gone."

A hard-working type, the British bicycle thief – overtime, late shifts? No problem. Last year, the police counted more than 100,000 stolen bikes, but it is estimated that for every theft recorded, four more go unreported – the true figure may be as high as half a million. That's about one bike every minute of the day, every day of the year.

What that tells you is that there is basically no bike lock that is completely proof against a determined bike-robber armed with bolt-cutters, hacksaw, liquid nitrogen and lump hammer, or even an angle-grinder. But you can at least give yourself a chance of finding your bike where you left it by following a few simple rules. First, lock up to an immovable piece of street furniture. Forget cable locks – they're little better than a bungee cord – a good D-lock or chain with padlock is what you need. And let price and weight be your guide: buy the best you can afford and the heaviest you can bear to carry.

The good news is that Stücke was soon reunited with his bicycle. Little more than a day after it had gone missing, it was recovered from a park. Presumably, the thief had realised that the resale value for this "old clonker", as Stücke describes it, was limited. The weird double handlebars and the piece of plywood showing a map of the world fitted into the frame are interesting variations on the way cycle couriers "distress" their bikes to deter thieves by wrapping old inner tubes around them.

The moral of the story is that the best defence against the brilliant British bicycle thief is to ride a bike that no one would possibly want. Still, I would advise Stücke to steer clear of Islington. There, as they say, anything goes.

Wednesday November 2, 2005

I love this statistic, always have. "On average, London commuters get wet fewer than 12 times a year." I've often quoted it to people myself, to be met with looks of disbelief and ridicule. It must, one feels, fall into the category of "lies, damned lies and statistics". Admittedly, October's weather was exceptional, but there are periods in winter when I'm sure I get wet 12 times a week, let alone a month. And commuters in cities such as Manchester and Glasgow will be laughing up their Gore-Tex sleeves at the idea of soft southerners braving a mere 12 days a year of cycling in the rain. But then it is, as we know, grim up north.

The 12-times-a-year stat comes courtesy of the London Cycling Campaign, recycled to coincide with the news from Transport for London that cycle use has doubled in the capital in the past five years. There are lots of claims for the credit: more and better cycle routes, improved parking facilities, the congestion charge and increasing cost of other means of transport, the "safety in numbers" effect of more cyclists on the road and, latterly, the fear of terrorism. The net effect is that the mayor's target of increasing the number of cycle journeys by 80% has been more than met five years ahead of its 2010 schedule.

A cause for celebration, time to crack open the champagne? You might think so, but that would be to underestimate the innate propensity of cyclists to snatch defeat from the jaws of victory. The truth is, cycling just wouldn't be any fun if we couldn't grumble about it. In this case, the complaint I'm hearing from the hardened veterans of city commuting is that all these latecomer cyclists don't have a clue about how to ride. They overtake you on the inside, push past at the lights, seem entirely oblivious to the Highway Code and – worst of all – can't even repair a puncture.

And now we know that it's no good hoping they are just fair-weather bikers if there are only 12 days a year when they decide to catch the bus instead. So, you see, every silver lining has a cloud.

Wednesday September 13, 2006

It had never occurred to me that there is such a profession as traffic psychologist. But, of course, there is. And there probably ought to be more of them. Our behaviour as road users is incredibly subtle and complex, yet most of it occurs unconsciously, without us even being aware of why we act in certain ways and what governs our decisions.

Only occasionally does something prompt a realisation of the sort of judgments I make automatically all the time. For example, there are some districts I cycle through where I am extra vigilant for hazards such as people opening car doors or double parking or doing U-turns. That may be rational in the sense that these are major shopping and market areas, with fewer drivers who are commuters or who drive for a living. But these may also be neighbourhoods with large ethnic minority populations. So what am I saying: that the drivers are worse in these districts? That begins to look a lot like prejudice.

Truth is, we make value judgments about other road users around us all the time – and we need to, because being able to predict their behaviour makes us safer. But, while we think our assessments are based on sound observation and experience, what if it is really all just blind prejudice?

To answer that question, I am now indebted to Dr Ian Walker, a traffic psychologist at Bath University. As widely reported yesterday, he has researched the effect of helmet use on cyclists' safety. We know very well the theory that says wearing a helmet can make cyclists indulge in more risk-taking than they otherwise would. But Walker has looked at helmet use from a completely new angle: not the cyclist's psychology, but the motorist's. In short, he has discovered that drivers perceive cyclists without helmets as more vulnerable and less competent than those with – and he knows this because he has measured how much extra distance they give the former when passing. On average, motorists will pass 85mm (3.3in) closer to you if you're wearing a helmet.

Fascinating stuff, with important implications. But there's more: Walker confirms that white-van drivers really are a menace: on average, they pass cyclists a massive 100mm (4in) nearer.

He also discovered that all drivers are sexist. Or chivalrous, depending on which way you look at it. When he wore a wig to impersonate a woman during his research, cars gave "him" a wider berth – by a whopping 140mm (5.5in) – because they thought they were passing a female cyclist.

Armed with this new knowledge, it is tempting to throw away the helmet, on the assumption that my cycling will be safer and more pleasant without. But I'm convinced helmets do prevent injury and save lives. I'm definitely thinking about getting a wig to wear under it, though.

Thursday December 14, 2006

Reasons to be a cheerful winter commuter. One: unlike the summer crush, you can usually find a place to lock your bike at work. Two: you don't arrive at your destination sweating profusely, covered in embarrassing damp patches and self-conscious about your malodorous T-shirt. Three: there is no three ... that's it.

Let's be thankful for small mercies, though. I rather like zipping up my snug jacket against the cold, sticking a fleece hat on, and donning my gloves as I pedal off. I know that last bit is quite possibly stupid. When I was a kid, my dad used to drive me mad by setting off in the car and only putting on his driving gloves (you can tell how long ago that was: who wears driving gloves now?) once already down the road – convincing this young passenger that a fatal crash was imminent. But there you go: like father, like son. At least I don't have any passengers to scare as I balance no-handed.

But it's the in-between seasons – and these very mild, global-warming days we're getting so many of now – where it's tricky. Do you go for the minimalist approach and accept that you'll shiver at first? Or do you wrap up and try to pedal slowly, but accept that you'll be sweltering in your own rainforest microclimate by the time you arrive? And is it just me who secretly quite likes the idea of the Gulf stream going into reverse, the coming of a new ice age and a bit of a snap in the air? The one thing we all hate is having to stop to take something off. I know I do, and if you think riding no-hands while I put my gloves on is foolhardy, you should see me taking a jacket off on the move.

Behind the clothing conundrum, however, lies a serious issue. A survey by the outdoor clothing company Rohan has found that 90% of people polled said they would consider cycling to work if they could freshen up before getting to their desks.

The 90% figure looks a bit suspicious to me, as it's one of those questions that begs a kind of "I'd be good if only I could" response. As in, 90% of people said they would put more of their earnings into savings if they were paid more. Not forgetting, either, the proprietary interest here in selling breathable outerwear.

But employers could do much more to encourage cycling by installing changing facilities, showers and lockers. I speak from personal experience: having changed department, I now find myself two floors from the nearest shower, and with nowhere to hang my towel. In London, several companies – the pharmaceutical giant GSK, for instance – have taken advantage of a matching-funding offer from Transport for London to put in facilities for cyclists.

It would be great to see more employers follow suit. If only to call the bluff of those nine-out-of-10 would-be bike-riders.

Thursday November 2, 2006

You know that something is afoot if bike parking is getting trendy. When architects and academics have decided it's time to wrest control of the humble cycle stand back from whatever obscure sub-discipline of industrial design it formerly belonged to and give it a makeover, something is definitely up.

So, banished will be the despised "butterfly" stand: cheap to instal but practically useless for holding up a bike and the cause of many a buckled wheel. Superseded is the "Sheffield" stand, that utilitarian inverted U of scaffolding pipe buried in concrete. From now on, bike stands will come in stainless steel or matt black only; and borough councils will be buying their "street furniture" from the Conran shop.

As if to prove it, the winning entry in a competition to design the next generation of bike parks, entitled Reinventing the Bike Shed, is called Habitat for Urban Bicycles (HUB – geddit?). The work of a Boston-based American architect, Robert Linn, this is an elegantly airy station where bikes are suspended by their front wheel, safely out of reach above the heads of passers-by, on a covered eliptical carousel. It is almost a visual joke: a glorified washing-line, but with bicycles instead of big pants swinging in the breeze. Key-code access would park your bike and see it returned to you by an automated "picker" system.

On aesthetic grounds, it beats the present look – that is, of massed ranks of rusting, skeletal remains no one would bother to steal. Small wonder people complain that bike parks are unsightly. But that's because the facilities we have are so blighted to begin with: open to the elements, vulnerable to thieves and inconveniently located.

Of course, any kind of storage creates problems. Another of the design entries posits what is, in effect, a very large closet, to provide a vertical solution to the bike park problem. In Amsterdam, where as many journeys are made by bike as by car, the need for mass provision has driven the development of the multi-storey bike park. It's not much prettier than a car park, but at least it's smaller. Of course, this opens up the very real risk of the cycling equivalent of that defining experience of auto-culture anomie: forgetting where you left it. We should be so lucky to live in a place where the plenitude of bicycles made that possible, but we could do better.

Linn's instinct for an aerial display seems apt. From its earliest days, the bicycle has been associated with flight and the sensation of flying. Another finalist in the competition, to follow the metaphor, is David Eburah's futuristic Placycle, in which bikes float in capsules above a central pod. Apparently, "ionisation" would provide the lift for this sea-anemone-like structure. But if he can levitate my clunker this way, he deserves to win not just Reinventing the Bike Shed, but a Nobel prize. Still, it shows that even with as lowly and earthbound a subject as bike parking, set the imagination free and the sky's the limit.

Thursday October 26, 2006

I have been thinking hard about what I could say that might persuade you that cycling in the rain is actually great. Because, after many weeks of weird, globally warmed postponement, autumn seems finally to have arrived. At least the wetness, if not the chill. Which is to say that those of us who live in the eastern half of the country are now getting a taste of what it is like to be a cyclist in Wales, Ireland, north-west England and western Scotland – those regions on the weather map where the clouds always seem busy precipitating, instead of just sitting there.

"You get wet, and after that you just keep riding and it's fine," a cycling friend said to me the other day. This struck me as Pollyanna-ish to a degree or two past even my own tendency to half-fullism. What's so fine about getting soaked to the skin, I thought.

Because, no matter what you have laid out to purchase waterproof technical apparel, you will get wet. Whatever the proud boast of breathability made by your £150 Gore-Tex jacket, a 10-minute ride at anything more than an amble will leave you as hotly moist as though you had just stepped from the steam room at a Turkish bath. And I have yet to find a garment that has discovered a way to prevent capillary action making water run uphill inside your cuffs, so that you end up feeling as if you have just done the dishes with your sleeves rolled down.

And then there is the wet feet business. Is there any experience more perfectly calibrated to sink the human spirit than the sensation of water seeping into one's socks? Even if you are foresighted enough to take some dry socks with you, there is no dodging the fact that, for the return journey, you will have to submit your feet to the clammy embrace of sodden footwear. And what kind of a life is it, really, when you have to carry around a spare pair of socks all the time?

And not just dry socks. If you are going to be prepared for our fickle climate, you have to have a pair of waterproof trousers, jacket, gloves and some kind of overshoes or galoshes. It can take 10 minutes to get ready for a 10-minute journey – and you feel got up like a deep-sea diver. Not so fine.

It is amazing, too, to see how many people ride through the winter without mudguards. The effect of this is to fire, as from one of those hoses they use to scrub the outside of old buildings, a jet of cold water, grit and grime directly between the buttocks. This is the moment at which an unwillingness to compromise the clean lines of one's bike becomes decidedly self-defeating.

So how am I doing with talking up the joys of autumnal cycling? There is one good thing I can think of: it gets much easier to find a place in the bike park.

Wednesday August 23, 2006

On the whole, I've nothing against bike lanes. As long as I don't have to ride in them, unless they're useful and convenient to me, I tend to think that dedicated road space for cyclists is a good, rather than a bad, thing (even if we tend to lose our own demarcated space precisely at those points where it would really be worth having).

But as I went out for an early ride on Sunday morning, before it got too hot, I remembered another good reason for not using bike lanes. They are always full of broken glass. When I got honked at by a car because I was riding just outside the lane, even though, at 8am, he had the whole road to pass me, it was nearly enough to spoil my sunny mood. Drivers, clearly, can have no idea when they see a cyclist wobble in front of them that, quite a lot of the time, it's to avoid a patch of needle-sharp shards deposited by their broken headlights and windscreens. And one thing passing cars do very effectively is "sweep" all that broken glass to the side of the road, where we are supposed to cycle.

The sheer quantity of it is staggering. On average, about 6% of the UK's 32m vehicles will have to replace their windscreens every year: that's getting on towards 2m units, or 20,000 tonnes of glass. The RAC claims that 95% of the half-million units it replaces every year get recycled. But even if, very conservatively, we took that optimistically low-sounding 5% figure to stand in for all unrecovered roadside breakages, that would still be 1,000 tonnes of broken windscreen a year dumped on our roads, before we even get into smashed side windows, shattered headlamps and the rest.

There is some comfort to cyclists in the fact that tyre manufacturers have partially met the challenge of the typical cycling environment – a razor-edged screed of shattered silica. In the old days, you paid your money and took your choice between either a tyre with a soft compound that had good traction but would puncture easily, or one with a hard compound that would wear better but have less grip (especially in the wet). Now the technology has moved on, and Kevlar – the stuff bullet-proof vests are made from – reinforces tyre treads (it's a war out there, after all).

I didn't get a puncture on Sunday, so I suppose I shouldn't complain. But when I passed one of those street-sweeping machines, I felt like cheering. Perhaps it's something to say to the motorist next time you hear the old chestnut about cyclists not having to pay road tax (apart from repeating the equally old correction that what they pay is a vehicle tax, not a road tax): that cyclists do pay council tax – which helps to clear up all the mess made by cars.

Wednesday February 8, 2006

A bike has been my main form of transport for more than 20 years, and most of those have been spent negotiating London traffic. So, I asked myself, what could I possibly learn from a cycle training course?

Such is the arrogance of, ahem, middle youth. But training is now a boom business: last November, Cycling England awarded £1m to the Cyclists' Touring Club to deliver a scheme to train more than 1,000 new instructors, and set a new national standard for cycle training (to take over from the old "proficiency" test). So I set aside my smug self-assurance and went back to school.

I got in touch with my local provider, Cycle Training UK. Founded in 1998, this not-for-profit firm now has between 50 and 60 instructors. "Last year saw a huge expansion," says David Dansky, my instructor for the morning. Everything they do – from teaching the basics of riding a bike to adults who missed out, to taking whole classes of kids out on the road, to running maintenance courses – is designed to achieve a simple goal, says David: "More trips, more often, more safely."

After a questionnaire to check I'm not on any mind-bending meds, and a look over my bike to test its roadworthiness, we make for a quiet cul-de-sac where David takes me through a routine to establish whether I have mastered the basics of bike control. I pass this, so we set off on to the public highway, with David riding behind to observe me.

Even something as automatic as riding a bike becomes tricky when you are acutely self-conscious, I discover. It's like telling someone: "Just act natural." It is guaranteed to produce the opposite effect. I'm soon pulled over for a talking-to: I've been riding in the gutter and not looking behind enough.

"As a rule of thumb," David explains, "cars will leave the same amount of space as they pass you as there is between you and the kerb." But won't it piss off motorists unnecessarily if I'm in the middle of the lane? Not if you're checking behind frequently – that way, drivers can see you're not oblivious. "The key is that you are communicating to other road users," says David. "You need to realise that you can manipulate the traffic."

This was my eureka moment. It's not about being mindlessly assertive; it's about making yourself safe by being part of the traffic stream rather than hiding in the margins. I hadn't understood how my behaviour was subtly reinforcing my cyclist sense of self as a done-down victim. In practical terms, perhaps, I didn't learn a lot, but conceptually, it was a major change of gear, a whole new mindset. I am now an arch-manipulator of traffic. And you know what? It feels good.

THREE

NUTS AND BOLTS: BECAUSE WE LOVE THE HARDWARE

An expat Brit I met in Vermont, New England, a few years ago told me, "You're not a proper cyclist if you don't collect a new bike every year." He was joking, of course, but only partly. I probably manage my addiction by keeping it to a new bike every couple of years, though even that requires a degree of subterfuge in hiding one's compulsive bike acquisition habit from one's family that only alcoholics or serial adulterers would recognise.

By new bike, of course, I do not necessarily mean a shiny, off-the-peg purchase. One of the pleasures of owning more than one bike is imagining and working out new ways of reconfiguring old bikes with different components. In the old days, when virtually all bikes were made of steel, and when a handbuilt frame was an invest-ment for at least a decade's use, people would treat themselves to sending off their chipped and road-soiled steed for a "respray" – a makeover with a fresh coat of paint and a new colour scheme. You'd almost feel you'd got a new bike when it came back and you built it back up. Even relatively recently, I turned an old touring frame into a fixed-wheel townie by having the ends of the rear triangle chopped off and track ends brazed on.

But such private projects are a dying tradition. As goes the rest of the world, cycling has become more and more consumer-oriented: the ethic of recycling bicycles abandoned in favour of a discard-and-buy imperative. Even many components now conform to the new mandate: they're not designed to be maintained, just used and chucked out when they wear out.

Still, the consumer revolution came late enough to cycling, and I should hardly complain: bike shops are infinitely more inviting places to visit now, the choices and the service vastly improved on the old tradition of ill-favoured offhandedness that characterised the proprietors of all too many of the old-fashioned shops – with the noble exception, of course, of the type who would mend your puncture and refuse to take money for doing it.

Judging by the condition of some bikes I see on the road, I have to confront the fact that there are some cyclists for whom a bicycle is merely a contraption made of metal and plastic for personal conveyance. But I find it quite hard to visit that way of thinking, as I long since passed over to the, I hope, much larger club of cyclists who have some sense of just what a perfect and pretty machine the bicycle is. I concede that, in extreme cases, it is possible to turn bikes into unhealthy fetish objects, but if you can't see the beauty of the bicycle, I would beg you to look again.

Wednesday September 14, 2005

I can still remember a time in my life when a large slice of my disposable income went on buying clothes. Lunch-hours often saw me making secretive sorties to favourite stores. The result was a wardrobe I couldn't afford, but that had some nice things in it.

And most of them I still have 15 years later. But nowadays, apart from the odd pair of jeans, I hardly buy clothes at all. Instead, whatever small portion of my income still remains – after household bills and kids' expenses have wreaked their monthly financial havoc – gets spent in bike shops. I simply love them. And judging by the queues at the tills, I am not alone. Rarely a week goes by without me finding some plausible but spurious reason – the need for a new brake cable or spare inner tube – to visit one.

It's a bit like the appeal of a good hardware shop. There's just all this great stuff. I won't pretend I've read much Heidegger (or any, in fact), but I'd like to think Martin had just spent a happy half-hour in Freiburg's bike shop when he was struck by "the thinginess of things". There it is, a cornucopia of exquisitely machined alloys, lustrous carbon-fibre frames, and innumerable form-fitting garments in hi-tech fabrics. Things don't get much thingier than this.

Once upon a time, bike shops were intimidating, lugubrious places. Only two interactions were possible. Either you would be made to feel very small by a spotty assistant ill-concealing his contempt that you did not know the name of the part you needed. Or you would be handed back a repaired bicycle by a sweaty guy who would have left black thumbprints all over your pride and joy.

Times have changed: the retail revolution came late to the cycle trade but it got there in the end. Hectares of high street space are now devoted to all the high-end kit – with hefty price tags attached. There's a glossy new world of "bike porn" out there. And I'm a sucker for it.

And yet ... *nostalgie de la boue* maybe, but the perverse thing is that there is a bit of me that misses the old bike shop, with its dusty displays, maladjusted staff, and eternal bin of nonmatching nuts and bolts. Punters! There's no pleasing them.

Wednesday April 12, 2006

I had one of those archetypal roadside experiences a couple of weeks ago. I was on a favourite weekend ride, down to Box Hill in Surrey. (There's a great Richard Thompson song about riding to Box Hill, by the way, 1952 Vincent Black Lightning – only it's about being on a motorbike, sadly.) It had rained the night before, and flints must have been washed on to the road, because I got a puncture.

Never mind, I had my mini-pump. But I hardly ever use it, so I'd forgotten how rubbish it was. Ten minutes of cramp-inducing pumping later, I had just enough air in the tyre to get home. This is too silly, I thought: I need one that works. So, armed with this more-than-adequate excuse, I went shopping.

The pump I have now, let me tell you, is about the size of a Cuban cigar (and cost as much, too). But it works brilliantly. And, best of all, it's lustrous black and made of carbon fibre.

There is now nothing on a bike or for a bike that cannot be bought in carbon fibre. Where once cyclists were seduced by chromed steel, aluminium (brushed or anodised), and the muted silver of titanium, now we want carbon-fibre everything – from the soles of our cycling shoes to the ends of our handlebars. And we'll pay a premium to get it. No wonder carbon is known in the trade as "black gold".

Admittedly, it's still all high-end stuff, but the prices of carbon-fibre frames have been coming down. You can buy a well-specced carbon road bike for under £1,000 now. Last year, one cycling magazine (probably thinking mainly of its male readers) asked: "What's a bigger turn-on, a carbon-fibre bicycle or silk lingerie?"

The original carbon fibre was patented by Thomas Edison in 1879 as a filament for electric lights, but industrial production of "composites" – woven fibres set in resin – was only perfected in the 60s, and has since been refined to reduce its environmental impact. The resulting material has spectacular properties: almost three times the tensile strength of toughened steel but at about a fifth of the weight. One Chinese manufacturer that makes bike frames for Giant used to use the stuff to build missiles. Carbon fibre, you might say, really is rocket science.

Which is largely why there is currently a "carbon-fibre famine". Between them, the Pentagon, Boeing and Airbus are vacuuming up all the world's available supply. Ironically, the other major industrial use is in the manufacture of prop blades for wind farms. Swords and ploughshares, indeed.

It does bother me that we're just bringing more plastic into the world. But if it's tougher than steel, that shouldn't matter because it will last. Who knows? Perhaps, in 100 years, carbon-fibre bikes will be as collectible as Bakelite ashtrays are today.

Thursday January 18, 2007

A thought occurred to me as I was hosing the mud off my cyclo-cross bike for the umpteenth time this winter: whatever became of my cone spanners?

A sad thought, in many ways. Sad, quite possibly, in the sense that standing around regretting the passing into obsolescence of cone spanners might be a sign that I should get out more. But sad, too, in the sense that it was a reminder of changing times and values.

The very fact that you can hose a bike clean and not live to regret it is a sign of how things have changed. A decade ago, you would not have dared take the jet-wash approach to cleaning your bike, no matter how dirty. It would have been a bucket of soapy water, a brush and sponge, and sleeves rolled up. Why? Because the idea of high-pressure water getting into the vital bearings of your bike – wheels and cranks – and stripping away the grease would have made any self-respecting cyclist recoil in horror.

This is where cone spanners came in. At least once a year, you would need to strip down your wheel bearings, clean them, repack with fresh grease, and reassemble. The bearings were not exactly open to the elements – the cups that held the ball bearings in place were occluded – but they were not, as they are today, virtually sealed units. Dust, grit and moisture could, and would, get in over time. And if you held up a wheel by its axle, span it and heard a ghastly gritty churning, you knew that maintenance was overdue.

And the cone spanners were what you needed for the job. The cones in question held the ball bearings in place against the cups, and the reassembly was a delicate business: over-tighten the cones and the bearings would not run freely; under-tighten them and the whole apparatus would have too much "play" in it, making the wheel rim wobble from side to side. It is a simple enough piece of mechanical craft, but doing both wheels was half a Saturday afternoon's work. And who has that sort of time now?

Instead, bearings are sealed and modular. I don't even know what they look like internally, and you wouldn't get very far trying to find out with a cone spanner, because there's no nut to get a purchase on. If the unit wears out, you just chuck it away and slot a new one in. In this cash-rich, time-poor epoch, no one is interested in maintaining or mending things, so bike bits have become disposable.

And, it has to be said, better. Do I honestly miss the fact that getting the muck off my bike used to take three or four times longer because it was a less robust creature? No, but progress always comes at a price. And today's casualty is the humble cone spanner: bound for oblivion on the scrapheap of bicycle history.

Monday April 3, 2006

The Question: Will Clive Sinclair's new folding bike work?

Well, he certainly thinks so. Sir Clive expects to sell 100,000 of his A-bikes in the first year after its launch in July. But the visionary entrepreneur's record of success is so mixed that predictions are tricky. Will the A-bike be a technological triumph, like Sinclair's revolutionary electronic calculator and Spectrum computer? Or will it turn out a well-intentioned turkey, like the C5 – Sinclair's three-wheeled electric buggy, which proved to be a spectacular flop and cost its inventor millions?

Let's take a closer look. There's a lot Sinclair gets right: the A-bike weighs only 5.5kg (little more than half most bikes); its chain is completely enclosed (so no more trousers ruined by grease marks); and it folds up in 15 seconds (whereas most folding bikes demand an NVQ in mechanical engineering). So maybe the A-bike is just what urban commuters – the park-and-ride crowd or rush-hour train travellers – need. Sinclair might just have cracked it.

But hold on: if this is a bike, where are the wheels? Oh, those are the wheels. I'm sorry to sound a bit trad, but aren't six-inch wheels for scooters? There is a practical difficulty here: small wheels tend to fall down holes and not climb out of them. The ride of the A-bike on anything less smooth than, say, a snooker table is likely to be bone-jarring at best. And when I last looked, our city streets were not paved with green baize. Sinclair's ingenuity is admirable, but trying to improve such a successful technology as the bicycle is like, well, reinventing the wheel.

The biggest problem, though, is not practical but aesthetic. Sinclair's transport contraptions always look as if they have been put together from the parts bin of the BBC workshops where they build the Daleks. Will anyone be seen dead riding one of these? Most people will work hard to avoid becoming a laughing stock. Sadly, Sir Clive does not seem to have the same threshold of social embarrassment as most people.

Wednesday April 19, 2006

If you ask people what their favourite bike tool is, most will say "the telephone". Reasonably enough, they have no wish to cover their hands with grease. No such issue arises with a numeric keypad: bike needs a service? Call the shop and book it in.

Bicycle maintenance is more a cult than an art; its mysteries and rites will never be more than a minority fetish. Yet we maintenance maniacs are cushioned from the full, lonely realisation of our weirdness by the mechanically inept majority's generous, if self-serving encouragement of the delusion that our ability to fix bikes has some social value. At least, that is the feeling I get when a colleague asks me to fit a light bracket or fix the indexing on their gears. Journalist by day, bicycle repair man by lunch-hour.

In fact, we have an honourable history. If it weren't for machine-sympathetic folk such as us, cyclists would still be going around in constant danger of their pedals falling off. Fortunately, a century ago, two bicycle mechanics from Dayton, Ohio, realised that the left-hand pedal needed to have a left-hand thread so that it self-tightened. To me, that was the Wright brothers' greatest invention. (If Kitty Hawk had ended up a rusting, skeletal heap in Wilbur and Orville's backyard, I'm not sure we wouldn't all have been better off.)

There are plenty of other nominations for the bicycle's most useful innovation. A Belfast vet, John Dunlop, might claim credit for his pneumatic tyre, but I am a fan of the Frenchman Eugene Meyer, who in 1869 invented wire spokes. Talk about reinventing the wheel: it became amazingly light yet as strong as ever. It had a degree of compliance that hugely improved handling and comfort, yet was rigid enough to transfer pedal power into forward motion with superb efficiency.

And that is why my favourite tool is the spoke key. For a wheel to be healthy, it should be "true" – run straight, without warp or wobble, its spokes evenly tensioned. Learning to true your own wheels is the most satisfying of accomplishments. If you ever do a maintenance class, this is the task to learn. Expert wheel-builders are craftsmen par excellence yet the basic principle is simple: tension the spokes on one side of the wheel to pull it one way; tighten the opposite side to pull the other. It's all about balance.

The best moment is when you've done your spoke-key tweaking and the wheel looks straightish. But you can't know for sure until you've stressed it – and the only real way of testing this is to ride on it. Then there's a lovely "plink, plonk, plunk" progression of the spokes adjusting to their new tensions, like impromptu tuning forks. For cyclists, that's the music of the spheres; and a true wheel the key to happiness.

Wednesday October 19, 2005

I just spent rather more on a spiffy pair of wheels for my racing bike than most people would think of spending on an entire new bicycle. (Oh, the wicked temptation of 0% finance, with its deliciously emollient way of turning an indigestibly large three-figure number into more palatable bite-sized monthly chunks.)

For anyone who went to this weekend's Cycle Show in east London, this may not be surprising. As you would have discovered if you had visited the cavernous halls of the ExCel exhibition centre beside the Royal Docks, it is quite possible to dispose of several thousand pounds on a bike. You could buy a car for that. And funnily enough, one choice item was a titanium, carbon and aluminium racing bike manufactured by the specialist Dutch firm Spyker, better known for making a low-slung, sculpted sports car that leaves car-mag types slack-jawed and salivating helplessly. The bike's price tag? 10,000 euros. We are talking bike bling here, big time.

But for even the most ardent cycle fetishist – and as I own, at the last count, six bikes, I'd probably have to put my hand up – there is something queasy about all this lustrous stuff. It's not just the kid-in-the-chocolate-factory feeling that you can have too much of a good thing; it is also that, deep down, you feel that cycling should be about something different from the world of conspicuous consumption – this reckless merry-go-round of marketing not to our needs, but our lusts.

How do you square saving the planet with satisfying your desire for a bike whose performance would be more than adequate for Lance Armstrong (which means, bluntly, it's too good for you)?

I've thought long and hard about this. Finally, I realised that we need bike bling. Imagine the poverty of life without glitzy cycle shows and £6,000 bikes. If it is ever to shake off the image of scruffy eccentricity and its third-class-passenger status, cycling must have this sort of investment and glamour. We'll never save the planet with bicycle clips alone. Convinced? Me neither.

Thursday March 8, 2007

Michael Killian definitely looks the part, right down to the handlebar moustache. Although he works as a software engineer in the US, the 46-year-old from Dublin is an inventor, one who has come up with a quite radical redesign of the bicycle.

What's new and different about it, you ask. Well, it still has two wheels, a saddle, pedals and handlebars, so it can't be all that radical, can it? Well, except that it's sideways. Which is to say that the bicycle still goes forwards in line with its wheels, but its rider sits at right angles to the direction of travel, and pedals crossways, too. It looks pretty nutty, as you can see for yourself if you visit Killian's site (sidewaysbike.com).

This is something of a departure. Since its earliest days, about 150 years ago, with the high wheelers that preceded the "safety bicycle" and what we would recognise as something very close to the modern bike, the bicycle has placed its rider facing forward, balanced symmetrically over the axis formed by the wheels. This was a template established even before the penny-farthing, with the genesis in the late 18th century of the freewheeling "hobbyhorses" and, later, "draisiennes" (like bikes but without pedals). At a stroke, then, Killian's invention overturns more than two centuries of engineering consensus about how personal travel could be accomplished without putting oats in one end and producing manure at the other; or latterly, petrol or diesel and noxious fumes.

Perhaps the first question is: "Does it work"? Well, Killian can ride it, according to the video evidence (unless his real talent is with computer graphics). But it is not as easy to control as the bike we have come to know and love; he admits that only about six out of 10 people seem able to master the counter-intuitive skill of sideways cycling.

The second and larger, philosophical question is "Why?" Killian is clearly enamoured of the experience, but the public is sceptical. While its inventor is convinced of its appeal to the cyclist "seeking more artistic expression in a bicycle", he has yet to find a manufacturer willing to put it into production.

Perhaps the lesson for us is that while the modern bicycle is a wonder of modern design, materials and manufacturing, in its essence – the "diamond frame", chain drive, wire-spoke wheels and pneumatic tyres – it has remained unchanged for well over a century. Everything, from derailleur gears (more than 60 years old) to disc brakes, is about improvement and refinement. Now and again, a major development comes along – clipless pedals, say – that soon supersedes an older technology (toeclips), but this is evolution, not revolution.

It would be complacent to say that revolutionary innovation is inconceivable. Cycling has always attracted more than its share of inventors. Remember Mike Burrows who, with Lotus, designed and built the remarkable aerodynamic bike on which Chris Boardman broke records and won gold at the Barcelona Olympics. Burrows is also the reason why practically all modern racing bikes have abandoned the old horizontal top tube in favour of the "compact" geometry of a tighter lozenge shape – arguably not as pretty, but undeniably effective in a sport where lightness and rigidity are what count.

But a sideways bike? That could be one turn of the crank too far.

Thursday February 22, 2007

There's one big problem with the fact that more of us are getting around by bike: more of us are having them stolen. If the bicycle trade is booming, so too is the black market in nicked bikes. Figures out recently from the insurer Direct Line suggest that a bike is stolen in the UK virtually every minute, totalling more than 400,000 thefts a year. Reliable figures are hard to come by, not least because police believe only about a quarter of thefts are reported. Previous estimates of the total figure have varied from 300,000 to half a million a year.

Besides the obvious distress, there are many depressing aspects to this modern curse of velo-kleptomania. One is that the police quote a recovery rate of a mere 5%. This is probably an overestimate: the clear-up rate has been documented, in some urban areas, to be as low as 2%. If you've ever had the experience of reporting a bike theft to the police, you will get the distinct impression that the only point was to get a crime number to authenticate your insurance claim.

Naturally, the acceleration of bicycle theft has also fuelled the number of claims and, consequently, the cost of premiums. It's reasonable to say that if you choose to insure your bike, you will have paid the full price of replacing it within about five years. A cheaper alternative is to rely on home-insurance cover, but these policies have a low cap on what you can claim and a high excess.

The hidden effect of bike theft is that it works as a significant disincentive: survey data show that two-thirds of people cycled less often, and nearly a quarter gave up altogether, after having a bike nicked. Part of this can be explained by the fact that more than half of cyclists do not have insurance, so individuals are taking the main hit of the estimated £35m annual cost of losses.

And this hides a huge trade in stolen goods. In London, I've occasionally heard of intrepid types getting up early on a Sunday morning to go to Brick Lane market and wrest their beloved machine back off a stallholder. It would be easy to condemn unscrupulous market dealers, and even the police who seem to turn a blind eye to this "informal economy", but the truth is that if you've ever bought a second-hand bike, you've probably been the final link in the chain of a "fencing" operation.

Have I? Yes, I've bought from a dodgy shop a bike which I knew was almost certainly stolen. What can you do? I asked for a receipt and got one. If I hadn't bought it, someone else would have. It's a form of crime that no one seems very interested in preventing.

Jenny Jones, the adviser on green transport to the London mayor, is an exception. She would like to run a different version of Direct Line's recent experiment of leaving locked bikes out and seeing how long they lasted (Croydon was worst in the UK; its decoy went within the hour.) Jones wants to see "baited" bikes used, with tracking technology, so that some proper police work would be done on bike theft for a change.

It's an appealing idea, if only to see some justice dispensed. But it doesn't tackle the root of the problem, which is that the bicycle industry itself has conspicuously done diddly-squat. The trade does very nicely, thank you, by linking up with the insurance companies to replace stolen bikes. Compare and contrast this with the efforts of mobile phone and car companies to tackle the issue: car theft, in particular, has fallen markedly. Witness the fact that the UK's most stolen car now is the Vauxhall Belmont. That's like saying the most stolen bike is a 20-year-old Raleigh. If only.

Thursday January 11, 2007

It started some time last week. A small click, or creak, when I pedalled. I tried to ignore it, hoping it would go away. And it did – intermittently. Then it would come back.

I knew I'd have to deal with it, but wasn't in a rush. Creaking noises from around the bottom bracket (which houses the main axle) are notoriously difficult to diagnose and fix. The last time I got a new bike, it had a BB creak. I took it back after a few days, and the shop's mechanic stripped down the unit and refitted it after giving everything an extra layer of lubrication. It's not uncommon, apparently, to get this phenomenon with aluminium alloy frames and the steel cups – the two different metal faces protest at meeting, and sometimes even a buffer of lithium grease can't soothe the initial frisson. In my case, it did seem to be sorted, until I went out on a very hot day and it started creaking again. But then it seemed to bed in, and the creaking stopped. Go figure.

Creaking is bad enough. But nothing gets under your skin like squeaking. There are two common sources. The first is a dry chain. I daily pass commuters riding bikes with squeaking chains. It's a crime against bikes; you should be able to report it to social services. I want to say, "Haven't you heard of oil?" or, more desperately, "Please oil your chain." But the honest truth is that I find the sound so painful – worse than fingernails being dragged across a blackboard – that I hurry on by. But they're going to bike hell, those people.

The other common squeak comes from dry jockey wheels. These are the two small plastic pulley discs that guide the chain through the derailleur mechanism. There's more excuse for letting these go dry than there is for running a dry chain. Being plastic, they don't need as much care and their crude roller bearings are not going to suffer much for lacking lube.

But when they squeak, they sing like a canary. About a year ago, I rode from London to Canterbury, the route of stage one of this year's Tour de France. My jockey wheels started squeaking somewhere around Erith, along the Thames estuary. I had to find a bike shop in Gravesend and beg for a squirt of WD40 because the prospect of going another 100 miles with that singsong twitter was more than my sanity would have borne.

A loved bike is a quiet bike. When they are working well, bicycles should be almost silent, emitting just a low hum, a purr of mechanical contentment.

So my creak? I found out what it was on Sunday morning, I'm ashamed to admit, when the left crank started to fall off. (Fortunately, I had a toolkit on board.) But the lesson is, listen to your bicycle: it may be trying to tell you something.

FOUR

GETTING IN GEAR:
CRUCIAL QUESTIONS
OF AESTHETICS

*It is a natural enough mistake to think of cycling as a purely phys-
ical activity, but to do so is to miss a vital dimension of the
experience of riding a bike: it is certainly a practice in aesthetics,
and quite possibly a spiritual exercise as well. It is normal when
considering any other sport or pastime – from riding a horse to
swinging a golf club – to think about the form and grace involved,
and to aspire to do it well and look good doing it. Perhaps because
we have become so accustomed to the bicycle being a humdrum
daily workhorse, and perhaps because the rider partly has the sense
of being entrained to a machine, it is easy to forget that cycling is
an action that can be done either well or badly.*

*As with any physical motion, cycling should look effortless and
fluid. Even when the effort is intense, there should be an easy
rhythm, a natural cadence, that lends harmony to the bicycle's
unique blend of human and machine. You watch a great stylist on
a bicycle (the only possible advice here is to advise finding some
archive footage of* il Campionissimo, *Fausto Coppi), and what*

you witness is a living incarnation of "the still point in the turn-ing world" of which TS Eliot wrote: "Except for the point, the still point, / There would be no dance".

Enough pretension: once you've acquired a sense of why it matters not to look a clod on a bike, the rest is shopping. And thank God we have more or less passed out of the era of DayGlo and fluo-rescence. Now that anything bike-wise can be made or covered or trimmed with lustrous reflective silver, the visibility argument falls and there's really no excuse for the eye-offending nature of bygone cycle apparel. The only question that then remains – for the male cyclist, at least – is whether to shave your legs. But that's another, as-yet-unwritten column.

Wednesday June 14, 2006

I believe I could sweat for Britain. And a bicycling problem I confess I have no solution to is how not to arrive in a ball of perspiration at the far end of my journey.

One way might be to wear cycling gear. You still sweat, but less – because the fabrics are thin and breathable. They do something called "wicking", if you believe the blurb on the label. This sounds vaguely pagan but is apparently a technical quality describing the garment's ability to transfer moisture away from the body. Bike-specific clothing is all very well for a long ride in the country, but around town I prefer to travel in civvies. Have you ever gone in to a high-street shop wearing a pair of cycling shorts? Self-conscious doesn't get near it. You might as well be in a tutu.

I am not a Lycra fetishist. I could wear shorts and T-shirt, like many others, but I find it a big drag to carry a change of clothes around. And swapping outfits when you get to work may be all right for commuters, but what about in the middle of the day when I often use my bike to get to meetings? On warm days, I just have to try to ride sedately enough not to turn into a wet rag after 10 minutes.

But on-bike temperature regulation is a more subtle and complex topic even than this. In the winter, you either have to judge your garmentry so that you're a bit too cold when you set off and grit your teeth until you warm up. Or you have to stop on the way to strip off a layer. Then there are those in-betweeny spring and autumn days when you're in two minds about what the "real-feel" temperature is – and no matter what you wear, it always seems to be the wrong thing.

Finally, there's the heatwave. However slowly you pedal, you're going to sweat like the proverbial. And the worst bit is that you can be riding along with the illusion that you're reasonably comfortable and cool, only to stop for traffic and suddenly discover that, without the breeze, you're drenched. At such moments, a sort of psychosis kicks in: even the water seeping across the road from a leaking main starts to look delicious, as if that yukky dribble were something you'd want to bathe in.

I spent Saturday afternoon riding around London – clothed – with protesters taking part in the World Naked Bike Ride. When I got home, I saw that my black T-shirt had collected tide-marks of exuded salt. Suddenly, naked made a lot of sense.

Wednesday September 6, 2006

I've been putting off writing this one. Not because it's a difficult or awkward subject, quite the reverse: because it's too pleasurable and feels as though I'm just boring on about a hobbyhorse. I think of it as "my paean to the fixed-wheel bike"

– a cycling topic that has to date seemed perhaps one click too arcane. But now I think it is no longer an indulgent fancy on my part, but an idea whose time has come.

What is a "fixed wheel", you ask. It is a bicycle pared to its essence: there are no gears but one, which means that there is just one chainring fitted to the cranks, just one sprocket at the back, and a single loop of chain tensioned between. Neither is there a freewheel mechanism, so you can't stop pedalling while the bicycle is in motion, because the momentum of the bike causes the pedals to rotate (independently of your force on the pedals making the bike go forward). Track bikes are still made this way, but once upon a time (circa 1900) all bicycles were fixed-wheel.

If you have never experienced riding a "fixie", it's hard to communicate adequately the almost transcendental pleasure of the sensation. Initiates of the art grow lyrical, even mystical, on the subject. On a fixed, you feel far more intimately "connected" to your bike. Your pedalling develops a silky smoothness; your legs benefit from greater "*souplesse*", as the French say. And let me not even get started on the joys of performing "track stands" – that is, balancing stationary on the bike (a relatively simple skill on a fixed) ... you begin to see why I've kept quiet till now. But perhaps I just wanted to keep it all to myself.

The only disadvantage is when you hit an incline. Still, a fixed is better than you would think on the hills: the way the bike's momentum pushes the pedals helps you over all but the most horribly steep with relative ease. And then there is the fact that a fixed-wheel bike has so few moving parts there's almost nothing to go wrong. Little to clean, little to wear out – it's the nearest you can get to a zero-maintenance bicycle.

Which explains its appeal to couriers. But the fixed has gone way beyond that subculture now. I see more and more commuters riding fixed-wheel bikes (or their vanilla cousin, the single speed with freewheel). And at the peripatetic Bicycle Film Festival, which opens for its second annual outing in London this week, there is a screening of Mash, a 20-minute film all about the fixed riders of San Francisco – a city whose hills, until now, have been more familiar in movies featuring car chases.

The fixed: practical, pleasurable, beautiful in its simplicity, and, as it happens, the last word in urban cool. What's not to like?

Wednesday November 23, 2005

Confession: I used to tuck my jeans into my socks. It was either that or wear bicycle clips. Whichever, let's face it, I had travelled deep into the realms of fashion solecism. Never mind whether you had on clean underwear or not, you wouldn't want to go under a bus wearing bike clips, would you? Or to be condemned to an eternity in the Elysian fields with your trousers tucked into your socks.

This raises the whole knotty question of what to wear on your bike. The "technical apparel" found in bike shops is incredibly advanced and does the job brilliantly. If you're going for a strenuous three-hour ride in the country, you are sorted: the sporty stuff is superb. But this still leaves the urban cyclist condemned to look like a plonker.

The problem is that if you're just pedalling to work or going down the high street to do a bit of shopping, you don't need hi-tech, man-made fibres with wonderful wicking features. What you want is something that won't spontaneously combust from static while you wait at the checkout. That's if you haven't already died of shame from queuing in figure-hugging polyamide.

But let's put "men in tights" gags to one side. My moment of revelation came when I realised I was no longer tucking my jeans in; I was rolling them up. Why? The answer is that you only have to look around. Unconsciously, I was copying what couriers do. Bike messengers are the visionary pioneers of the cycling community. Where they go, others follow – just as the smart money in real estate always tracks artists. Wherever creatives colonise, cafes, galleries and restaurants soon follow: before you know it, paint-messed studios have become premium loft space.

So it is with cycle couriers: the way they dress – a blend of street-fashion and utility-cool – is the cutting edge. One day soon, someone will catch on and start selling us urban cyclists something both practical and chic – and I'll be first in line. Until then, I prefer my jeans rolled, not tucked.

Wednesday May 3, 2006

Panniers. Let's face it, they're not tremendously sexy, are they? They don't do much for a bike, looks-wise. Perhaps I'm prejudiced, but there are plenty of people, after all, who would rather get a wet bum than spoil the lines of their machine by fitting mudguards. I'm not quite of their number. Or rather, I've a foot in both camps – by having fair-weather bikes without guards, and foul-weather ones with. But I draw the line at a rack and panniers. I know they are immensely practical, but they just look so, you know, earnest.

Only if I were going on a serious cycle-touring holiday would I deign to bolt them to a bike of mine. Instead, for day-to-day use, I'd rather put up with almost any amount of stuff loaded into my bike bag – a completely frivolous preference that no doubt keeps my osteopath in business.

So I can't help but have a little sympathy for the Conservative leader, David Cameron, who has been skewered in recent days over the revelation that while he cycles home, in a show of seeming eco-virtue, his driver sometimes follows him in a car with his briefcase, papers, clothes and shoes. Cameron was somewhat stunned to be grilled on the subject by John Humphrys on the Today programme.

Humphrys revealed that he'd done his research and found online some vastly capacious panniers that could surely swallow Cameron's shadow-ministerial paperwork and his pair of Church's. It would only have been slightly more surreal if Humphrys had asked why the Tory leader had not brought back a sled and team of huskies from Norway to perform the task of commuting from Notting Hill to parliament. There's a photo op for you, Dave – "Then it was two jags, now it's two dogs." Take it and run with it.

Funnily enough, in a moment of despair about global warming and self-loathing for owning a car, I acquired a bike trailer last year. About every other week, I hitch it to my bike and do the supermarket run. I feel a bit of a twit, but actually it gets some admiring comments from other cyclists – usually the ones lugging panniers. It comfortably carries at least double what the biggest panniers could. And I kid myself that we might one day use it to go touring and camping. But its main attraction, frankly, is that it isn't a pair of panniers.

So I don't believe Cameron should have to answer to the pannier police. Yes, it seems a bit of a nonsense that there's a car following him occasionally, but would it make any difference if Cameron was in it, rather than riding his bike? The truth is he's a long-time cyclist. It's not a cynical parading of green credentials; he's on his bike because it's healthy and he enjoys it. And that, if not he, gets my vote.

FIVE

SPORTING PURSUITS:
IT IS ABOUT THE BIKE

I have tried to be aware, in these pieces, that I am writing chiefly for that putative animal, the general reader cyclist (or do I mean the general cyclist reader?). So I have been mindful of not riding too many of my own personal hobbyhorses. In the case of cycle sport, though, I seem to have failed comprehensively. But at least putting all the columns about one form of bike-racing or another in a single place allows those who find competition and sport repellent to skip the chapter.

For the rest, I realise that anything I say about cycle sport, being outside the sports pages, will probably seem thin fare. And anyone interested in the various sub-disciplines of mountain-biking will be thoroughly disappointed with me. It's a world within a world about which I wish I knew more, and which perhaps I will one day study closer.

But that is what all cycle sport is – a series of worlds within worlds. If I had a serious object in mind when writing about them, beyond communicating my own passionate interest and involvement, it was to give a sense of the rich and strange variety of ways people have found of competing on bikes. And what you discover when you enter one of these worlds, each with its unique traditions, customs and etiquette, is that the plain, common-sense matter of going fast on a bike is barely the half of it. A whole panoply of ritual, codes of honour and tactical complexity opens up.

And then, of course, there is the dark side. With over a century's history of performance-enhancing substance abuse, cycling has a deservedly notorious reputation for doping, to this day. As long as people are paid to race, and possibly not even then, drug abuse will be part of bike-racing. Any fan of cycling is obliged to be a dualist in their enthusiasm, believing in the reality of both good and evil in cycle sport.

What renews my belief, though, is the love and devotion I witness in the humble grassroots of the sport in which I participate and where the racing is pure at heart. All of us who race have our own dreams and ambitions, but here you find it is chiefly fun and fellowship. That you can believe.

Wednesday July 12, 2006

"It was epic. Six hours, 55 mins of hell. Lovely day though." So read the text message that came via France on Monday from my friend Guy. He had just completed l'Étape du Tour, the mountain stage of the Tour de France where they let some 7,500 amateurs loose on the same roads that the pros will ride a week later. This Étape was what will be stage 15, from Gap to Alpe d'Huez – the 14km climb legendary for its 21 hairpin bends.

The Étape has become an annual goal and red-letter day for thousands of cyclists. Riding on closed roads up and down the "monuments" of the Tour is the equivalent of your Sunday-league footballer playing at Wembley. As Guy's message neatly encapsulated, cycling more than 100 miles over some of

Europe's biggest mountains allows mere mortals to experience the extraordinary blend of agony and euphoria that makes the Tour the spectacle it is.

The beauty of the genre – which, on the continent, goes by the name of "cyclo-sportive" – is that these challenges bridge the gap between recreational riding and cycle sport, between charity rides and full-on road racing. Which is why their popularity is growing phenomenally. Besides the Étape, France hosts a summer-long series of cyclo-sportives. In Belgium, you can ride the routes of Spring Classics such as the Tour of Flanders or the Liège-Bastogne-Liège the day before the races themselves – usually with authentically gritty Belgian weather to make you even more grateful for the *frites* and beer later. Italy has the Gran Fondo series for those who want to explore the same Dolomite passes and Tuscan hills as the Giro d'Italia runs over. And the trend has even hit Britain with new events such as the Dragon Ride in Wales and the Etape du Dales in Yorkshire.

The bike manufacturers are getting in on the act, too, marketing what are essentially racing bikes but re-specced for greater comfort and easier gears. Tour operators are also gearing up: last week, as a guest of Sports Tours International (one of the companies that takes British riders to the Étape) and the upmarket cycle clothing maker Rapha, I joined a group of like-minded enthusiasts to ride stage 5 of the Tour on the morning of the race itself: 225km through beautiful, rolling Normandy countryside and, towards the finish, closed roads and crowds of cheering French fans. After all the depressing news about doping scandals, I felt the cloud of cynicism that had loomed over the Tour lift and blow away with the sea breeze at Caen.

When the Tour comes to Britain next year, we will have our very own Étape, a 130-mile cyclist's pilgrimage from London to Canterbury. I, for one, can hardly wait.

Wednesday June 28, 2006

The French call them "*chutes*" – a term so much more expressive than the old Anglo-Saxon. *Une chute* somehow gets at the experience in the way that that general-purpose workhorse of a word, crash, just doesn't. It captures the sense not only of the first jarring impact, but also of the sliding or skating down the road – tarmac-surfing (a phrase with a grim sense of humour as it makes something really unpleasant sound almost fun).

We have all fallen off our bikes from time to time. Unfortunately, "coming a cropper", as the penny-farthing pioneers used to call it, seems part of the deal. Generally, we get up, dust ourselves down and go on our way with our egos the most bruised thing about us. But a real crash, *une vraie chute*, is what happens at speed – a hazard chiefly of racing. Next week, the first week of the Tour de France, you will see plenty.

On the Tour, the best a rider can hope for is to escape with a nasty dose of "road rash": deep grazes raw to the touch and weeping for days. You see the riding wounded afterwards with gauze bandages taped to their limbs. But more serious damage is just around the corner: by the law of averages and long experience, it is predictable that a few unlucky riders will exit the Tour early with broken wrists, ribs or collarbones.

Crashes in amateur races are an ever present risk, but relatively rare. Two of my teammates went down last week. I was lucky: it happened just behind me – and all I caught was a glimpse of something going awry and then that sickening ring of metal and plastic clattering on tarmac. But a friend lost a couple of teeth – all because someone in front of him got his bars snagged on another rider and fell over.

The pros seem to crash more often, which seems mysterious: these, after all, are the best cyclists in the world. Week in, week out, they ride side by side in 150-plus groups over cobbles, through towns and over mountain passes. But in the Tour, the stakes are high: the pressure is on each team to deliver results for its sponsor; and every rider is thinking about where his next contract might be coming from.

The sprints that usually provide the finale to the flat opening stages are ferociously competitive, the speeds – 35-40mph – astronomical. Pushing and shoving is normal, as position is vital. All it takes, then, is for a touch of wheels or for a gap between riders and barriers suddenly to close, and then you have a spectacular. You will see it happen. And you will watch it again in slo-mo.

So spare a thought for the rider who will spend the next fortnight trying to sleep on the side that didn't get the cut-price dermabrasion job.

Wednesday August 9, 2006

The disgrace of Floyd Landis, disqualified from the Tour de France on Saturday and summarily sacked by his team, has been the only cycling story you could read for the past two weeks. And cycling's doping problem has been the only talking point. Shock, denial, anger, depression ... those of us who care about these things, have to endure the familiar sense of loss – loss of any heroes worthy of the name.

But overlooked in this sorry business is the fact that, if only we were not so blinkered by received values, we do still have a hero worthy of the name. And her name is Nicole Cooke.

While everyone has been looking the other way, the young woman from South Wales – long the best in Britain (national champion for the past seven years) – has recently consolidated her claim to be the best female bike racer in the world. Not only did she win the women's Tour de France this year (though it was virtually unreported in British sports pages), she has now established a commanding lead in the season-long World Cup rankings.

If you thought that in a sport demanding extreme endurance, fitness and speed, women would be the weaker sex, think again. A male friend who races as a top elite amateur told me that he went mountain-biking in the Brecon Beacons with a group including Cooke last winter – and she dropped him on every climb. She is, by any measure, a phenomenal athlete. And it goes without saying that she is clean of drugs.

So why is Cooke not a household name? Why isn't her picture on the back of cereal packets? There are no simple answers. In this country, women's cycling is a Cinderella sport within a Cinderella sport. Even in mainland Europe, it is the poor relation to the men's sport. Nothing unusual there; the rewards and coverage of women's tennis are the exception that proves the rule in almost every other sport.

And like many others, cycling is battling to turn round a history of disregarding women's participation. It is easy to throw about accusations of institutional sexism – and it is true that, in the bad old days, cycling clubs were not very welcoming towards potential female members. (Then again, some were not very welcoming, fullstop.) That is changing, but the larger truth is that sports simply reflect society.

More women are cycling than before; but even as commuting cyclists, men have tended to outnumber women by a factor of four or five to one. What goes into that? A perception that cycling is unsafe has deterred more women than men, probably; that bike shops are unfriendly places in a specifically sexist way, perhaps; that it is hard to dress nicely and ride a bike, possibly. But one excuse we can't make any more is a lack of role models. Not now that we have Nicole Cooke.

Thursday November 16, 2006

One of the things I love about cycle sport is that there are so many varieties: sports within a sport. For most of the world, perhaps, there is just the Tour de France every year in July and then some strange antics in a velodrome every four years at the Olympics. But competition goes on all year round, especially at the grassroots.

October and November are the months for hill-climb competitions: all over the country, the little 60-kilo guys get their hour – or rather, their three minutes – of glory by racing up the local landmark hill against the clock. Then, for the connoisseur of the truly arcane, there are roller leagues (sprint competitions on stationary bikes) and cycle speedway races. Indoor velodromes, too, stay busy and brightly lit through the dark evenings.

But the competitive spirit survives out in the fresh air also. I am a big disappointment to mountain bikers because their world of racing – from cross country to enduro events and downhilling – is a largely alien subculture to me; I don't know to report it. But the one area of substantial overlap is the winter sport of cyclo-cross. For this, mountain bikers and road racers alike abandon their machines of choice and adopt a kind of hybrid beast, which has a frame, handlebars and wheels like a racing bike, but brakes, gears and knobbly tyres more akin to a mountain bike.

I'm a late convert, but "cross" – as its devotees call it – has become perhaps my favourite cycle sport. It has a glorious simplicity, as all it consists of is charging about a muddy field for an hour. Typically, a course is laid out around a school playing field or suburban park, on which elsewhere your usual Sunday football games are going on.

Cross is a winter sport par excellence: gritty, physical, dirty. I was going to describe it as being a bit like rugby on a bike, but without the tackling – then I recalled that in the last race I did, I tangled with another rider and he ended up on the floor. Tricky off-camber corners and greasy surfaces, in any case, make falling off a constant hazard, but, generally, you land on grass or mud and you're not travelling that fast, so injuries are rare.

Cross can be harrowing at times, but it is also tremendous fun: for sheer kicks, the best I've had on a bike. The kind of activity that, afterwards, makes a mug of hot, sweet tea taste like the best drink in the world.

But best of all is the inclusiveness of cyclo-cross. It gathers up all ages, both sexes, and all abilities. The atmosphere has an informality and friendliness quite unlike the nervy clique-ishness of road-racing events. No one cares what you wear or what kind of bike you have. In fact, if you haven't got a cross bike, you can use a mountain bike. That's how inclusive it is.

Wednesday April 5, 2006

You don't come across cobbles much any more. Occasionally, you see a little patch of them showing through in a spot where the tarmac has broken up, which always makes me think of that line of TS Eliot's about "the skull beneath the skin". In fact, there is a little street behind the Guardian building, Back Hill, which is pure cobbles. It's steep, too, but with the bumps it's hard to say which is worse – going up slowly or down quickly. It's picturesque, but I tend to go the long way round to avoid it.

In Belgium, this is generally not an option. There, cobbles have never gone out of fashion. Only they're not called cobbles; it's *pavé*. In fact, the Belgians like their *pavé* so much, they have bike races organised specifically to go over the cobbles. Of these, the greatest is the Paris-Roubaix – also known as the Queen of Classics, the Hell of the North, La Pascale.

The association with Easter is appropriate (it takes place this Sunday). The Paris-Roubaix is the toughest, cruellest race in the calendar: though one-day only, it is harder in its way than the Tour de France. But like the Easter story, this epic of suffering has a redemptive theme. As the great Irish cyclist Sean Kelly (twice a winner) will tell you, it is the hardest race of all – and "the most beautiful to win". But, as he often found, it hurt to pee for three days afterwards.

The race begins in the flattish but rolling farmland of north-eastern France, traverses the mining region in which Zola's novel Germinal was set, and ends in an unprepossessing concrete velodrome in the industrial town of Roubaix. None of it is pretty, but that's not the point. The cobbles are the point, some sections dating back to the days of Napoleon. In dry conditions, you will see riders racing on the packed-mud shoulder rather than endure the bone-jarring *pavé*. But in the wet, the verge turns into a quagmire and there is no option but to bounce over the treacherously slippery cobbles.

The Paris-Roubaix takes no prisoners. When the Flemish rider Johan Museeuw won in 2000, he pointed to his knee as he crossed the line: after crashing on the cobbles the year before, he had contracted gangrene in the smashed joint – an incident that nearly cost him not only his career but also his leg. The grim purgatory of the race was memorably captured by the Danish director Jorgen Leth in his 1976 documentary, A Sunday in Hell: the riders looked like coalminers after a 10-hour shift as they scrubbed themselves down in the shower stalls.

The winner of the Paris-Roubaix gets not a trophy, but a lump of granite, which tells you all you need to know about the meaning of this race. No event captures cycle racing's strange romance with pain so well as the Paris-Roubaix. Perhaps I will ride up Back Hill on my way home, after all.

Thursday January 4, 2007

I'd be the first to admit that, as national championships go, it's not the most glamorous. The crowd at Southampton this week-end will number just a few hundred, even if it will try to compensate for its modest size with noisy enthusiasm. As for TV coverage, well, there'll probably be a few family members with DVD cameras to record the event. And the venue? A muddy field next to a sports centre somewhere on the south coast. Wembley it ain't.

Welcome to the obscure world of cyclo-cross. As minor sports go, it doesn't get much more minor than this. You'd be excused, in fact, for not having the foggiest what it is. Cyclo-cross is, in effect, a winter version of bike racing – but not on the road or a track. It's chiefly off-road, but it predates mountain biking, so the bikes look more like racing bikes, but with knobbly tyres for better grip on slippery, loose surfaces.

You race around a circuit, often in a park or on school playing field, for about an hour. Races have massed starts, so there's a tremendous scrum to get into the first corner or technical section ahead of your rivals. And then it's just a hard slog, often with the course getting more churned up, muddy and treacherous as the race goes on. Circuits often have obstacles designed or built into them: hurdles that require riders to dismount, run-ups or steps where you have to shoulder your bike, tricky descents or off-camber corners ... and plenty of mud. Top riders often have a spare bike to swap on to in the pits, with a helper on hand to scrub the worst of the dirt off each machine in turn.

It's a tough workout, fast and furious, physically demanding and testing of nerve and skill. It's a classic winter sport: sort of like rugby, but on a bike, without a ball, and, usually, without the physical contact. It's huge fun – and at the grassroots, its most appealing quality is that it attracts people of all ages and abilities, from youth, juniors, seniors, women and veterans. Cycle-racing is not always the most accessible sport, but in cyclo-cross it's at its most inclusive, friendly best.

So, on Saturday, I'll find myself lining up with 80 others for the veteran's (over-40s) event, before the main, senior men's, juniors' and women's events on Sunday. I certainly won't be in the running for a national jersey – if I finish in the top half, I'll be satisfied. But it's the event: a national champs is a national champs, after all, entitling the winner to wear a white jersey with red and blue hoops for the next year.

In the senior race, the reigning champion is Roger Hammond, who has carved out a successful career as a professional road-racer with the Discovery and now T-Mobile teams.

He is a former junior world champion in cyclo-cross, which would hardly make you a household name here, but in Belgium would earn you the right to free beers for life in many bars. There, the sport is huge, with thousands of fans, scores of professionals, and massive media coverage. It's been growing rapidly in the United States, too, after Lance Armstrong started showing up at cross races in the off-season.

Could that happen here? Unlikely. And perhaps, in truth, small is how we like it. There's something gloriously, wilfully eccentric about slogging round a muddy field in the midwinter murk – getting tired, sweaty, dirty and cold. But that hot bath never felt so well earned.

Wednesday July 5, 2006

"Pot Belge" sounds like something you might get after overindulging on Hoegaarden. Actually, it's a bit more potent than that. "Belgian mix", as it is generally translated, is a combination of amphetamines, cocaine and heroin. It's a cheap and dirty performance-enhancing drug for cyclists.

What's Belgian about it? Well, cycling is a huge participation sport there. All season long, you can race every day of the week on a "*kermesse*", a circuit race based around a village or small town. Local businesses put up the prize money, a few hundred euros. You can make a decent living even without being a full-time professional. The races are short, hard and fast; the testing regime haphazard. Hence "pot Belge": the winner's little helper.

While the Tour de France has been scandalised by revelations from Spain's "Operación Puerto" investigation into organised drug-taking and blood-doping for pro cyclists (leading to the suspension of two Tour favourites, Ivan Basso and Jan Ullrich), the news from a Bordeaux courtroom is just as grim. A former cycling coach, Freddy Sergant, has been jailed for running a ring that supplied Belgian mix; others received fines and suspended sentences.

Giving evidence, the former French pro Laurent Roux remarked that, at the top end of the sport, "Doctors cost more to hire than the riders." Much more depressing is that this sordid little drug bust shows just how far down the sport the doping problem goes – well into the amateur ranks. The pros do the hi-tech blood-doping; the aspiring amateurs ride on whizz till they can afford something better.

And "pot Belge" is not just a Belgian problem. As when syphilis appeared in the middle ages, everyone found someone else to blame: the French evil, the Spanish disease, the Neapolitan "bone-ache". The reality is that doping is universal and endemic in cycling. At least in mainland Europe.

Nobody will quite say it, but one reason why the most talented British riders never seem to realise their promise is that most stay clean. They don't come from a culture that accepts doping as the norm. The sport here is too small and there isn't enough money in it to make it worth people's while to buy the gear. Plenty of us do use legal ergogenic aids such as creatine, colostrum and sodium phosphate. I know the mentality: when you're taking supplements to boost perform-ance, it's very easy to blur the boundaries for yourself into a morally grey continuum.

Are we so ethically superior then? I never thought I'd say this, but let's hope the sport here stays so poor that we never have to find out.

Wednesday August 30, 2006

The Today programme is such an ingrained habit that I can't do without even the bits I hate – such as Thought for the Day and the sport. The sports coverage on Today is almost all football, usually the guy called Garry interviewing another guy called Garry in one of two modes: either alpha-male ferret or fawning puppy. If cycling gets mentioned at all at 25 past the hour, it's only during the Tour de France and then the chief interest is in how radically Garry will mispronounce the name of the previous day's stage winner.

But you see how the cynicism of the minority sport fan is rewarded. Yesterday, Today ran a long segment on the Tour of Britain, which has just begun (it finishes in London on Sunday). The gist was that while the top echelon of cycle sport is in desperate crisis, with major sponsors pulling out left, right and centre after getting burned with doping scandals, the lower orders are in rude health. As a participation sport, cycling is flourishing. A measure of the enthusiasm is that more than 1,500 people have volunteered to marshall the Tour of Britain, standing at junctions with flags to maintain the rolling roadblock so the riders can race safely on closed roads.

I've just been on holiday in Brittany, where cycling is a secular religion. For a cyclo-sportive in honour of a local hero, Bernard Hinault, with 600 entrants for a hilly 140m ride (despite a poor weather forecast), squadrons of motorcycle outriders performed the task of stopping traffic the whole way. Every Sunday, from Finisterre to Normandy and from Roscoff to the Loire, high streets and local roads are closed and whole villages turn out *en fête* for bike races. On our way home I read the regional paper, Ouest-France, which proudly proclaimed that 100,000 people had turned out to watch the professionals race at Plouay in last weekend's round of cycling's World Cup. And this despite the taint of *dopage* at the top of the sport.

Many like me have long been used to looking across the Channel, enviously thinking, oh well, of course: that's France. Cycling is truly popular there. But a great deal of it is to do not with popularity in the sense of mass participation – cycling is a minority sport even in France – but with promotion: how to put on an event with panache, how to create a sporting spectacle that anyone can enjoy and find colourful and exciting. This is what makes the Tour of Britain such an inspired effort. It's a work in progress, but it gets bigger and better every year. I'll be there to watch the finish on Sunday, and to do the grassroots thing by taking part in the amateur race beforehand.

But don't take it from me. Just ask Garry.

Wednesday January 25, 2006

Hurrah! London is to get a two-day visit from the Tour de France in 2007. The entire extraordinary cavalcade of 198 riders and several hundred team cars, press motorcycles, race officials' vehicles and bizarre promotional "floats" will process through the streets of London. And millions of people will turn out to watch the UK portion of one of the biggest sporting spectacles in the world. I say millions advisedly, because that is what happened the last time the Tour came to Britain in 1994. Ditchling Beacon – the hill that everybody who has done the London-to-Brighton ride knows as their nemesis – was transformed into a little Alp, with fans 30-deep on the hillside. It was a triumphal moment.

Next year's UK Tour stages will be bigger still. There is something special about the landmark roads of London being closed to traffic for a bicycle race, just as happens every year in Paris for the finale of the Tour on the Champs Elysées. The mayor of London, Ken Livingstone, deserves much praise for his vision in bringing the Tour back to Britain. His logic is straightforward: get more people on their bikes by making cycling exciting. First, bring the Tour of Britain to central London to test the infrastructure; next, host the Tour de France and expand the scale; finally, put the cycling events of the 2012 Olympics at the heart of London's strategy for making the games a success.

And the plan is working. Cycling is no longer a sport of socially challenged weirdos who meet on windswept dual carriageways in the early morning to discuss gear ratios. Actually, we still do, but now cycling is also mainstream and sexy – and, best of all, we're good at it.

But omelettes involve breakages. One of the ironies of the success of the 2012 bid is that the siting of the Olympic village on Hackney Marshes involves the razing to the ground of London's main cycle racing circuit, Eastway. In time, there will be a new velodrome as a legacy of the games, but from this year the redevelopment will mean the closure of a road circuit that just celebrated its 30th anniversary, and the loss of the only location inside the M25 where off-road racing is permitted (and cross-country mountain-biking is an Olympic event). Eastway has thousands of users: like many others, I race there virtually every week. The Olympic gold winner Bradley Wiggins also still makes occasional appearances.

In its haste to see the velodrome delivered, the sport's governing body, British Cycling, has connived at this closure without a satisfactory replacement being found or proper consultation. In the crucial five years before the Olympics, London risks losing its main venue for cycle sport.

But I'm still sanguine: I bet this is the kind of thing the mayor can fix before breakfast.

Wednesday February 22, 2006

It still feels like winter, although the crocuses pushing up in the garden seem to think it's spring. This optimism seems to be shared by racing cyclists, many of whom, like me, are dusting off their best wheels and getting ready for another season of competition.

Some pro teams have started already, in the warmer climes of Malaysia and California, but the European professional calendar does not get into gear until early March, with the Paris-Nice stage race. British amateurs are a hardy breed, however, and some started their racing more than a week ago at the traditional south-coast season-opener, the Perf's Pedal. The rain lashed down; there was so much muck on the roads that the riders who finished looked like coalminers; a couple of horses on the circuit were startled and bolted, causing several cyclists to crash (fortunately, without serious consequence). All in all, a classic British road race.

No wonder there are not many of us. The sport's governing body in the UK, British Cycling, was pleased to announce recently a 20% membership increase – up to about 19,000 in 2005. Of these, just over half take out a racing licence. In other words, this is a sport that, nationally, has at most 10,000 active participants. A friend of mine who runs a magazine company told me the other day that he publishes a title for polo players that has a print run of 20,000. Which suggests that, on any given weekend, there could well be more people chasing around a field on a pony trying to hit a ball with a mallet than there are people doing bike races. No disrespect to chukka fans, but this is a depressing thought.

I did my first race last Saturday and one of the pleasures was seeing familiar faces and renewing acquaintance with people I raced against last season, and the season before, and so on. If this subculture is a cosy niche where it feels as if you know everyone, that may be because, after a while, you actually do.

The paradox of this marginality is how amazingly good at producing world-class cyclists Britain is, considering we're up against countries such as France and Belgium where cycle sport is like a religion. In the UK, there is scarcely such a thing as a professional cyclist – which is why almost every British cyclist of talent and ambition goes abroad to pursue a career. The peculiarity of this situation should please my colleague Simon Jenkins, who last week attacked the idea of the Exchequer footing the bill for training our Olympic athletes, because many of our most successful cyclists (such as the triple medal-winner Bradley Wiggins) are on the payroll of French, German, Dutch or Italian teams. Beautiful, eh?

Incidentally, there is a version of polo played on bicycles. But getting enough players for a game isn't easy.

Wednesday May 24, 2006

It used to be said, back in the good old days when Channel 4 ran daily highlights of the Tour de France before its flagship evening news programme, that a substantial proportion of the audience tuned in not because they had any interest in the racing but because they liked ogling the fabulous aerial shots of French countryside. Maybe the viewing figures were more about fantasy second-home hunting than cycle-sport fandom, but who was complaining?

To get the Tour highlights these days, you either have to subscribe to Eurosport or watch ITV2 at dead of night. Only if you have satellite TV in North America can you get C4's old team of Phil Liggett and Paul Sherwen "in exile" for Canada's Outdoor Life Network.

Given cycling's resurgent popularity, non-subscription channels may be missing a trick by virtually ignoring the Tour de France. But even more frustrating and inexplicable to the cycling tifosi (fanbase) is the apparent media ban on the Tour of Italy – the Giro d'Italia. If you thought the fields of ripening sunflowers in France were picturesque, imagine the panoramic shots of the Ligurian coast, the Tuscan hills, the Julian Alps and the magnificent Dolomites.

The Giro suffered a bad patch in the late 1990s, when Italy was perhaps the nation worst affected by the doping scandals that shook professional cycling. Then it was sidelined by the dominance of Lance Armstrong: his all-or-nothing strategy of winning the Tour de France and the Tour alone meant that riding the Giro was simply not part of the plan.

But now the Giro is back. While the Tour often seems over-controlled and stage-managed, the Giro last year provided thrilling racing right up until the final stage. This year, Italy's Ivan Basso (Lance's most serious challenger in his latter years) looks unbeatable. If Basso carries forward that form, he must be favoured to achieve a Giro/Tour double not attained since Marco Pantani did it in 1998.

But there has been plenty of interest besides the leader: a stunning victory in a time trial for Jan Ullrich, a former Tour winner, boding well for his prospects in July after a lacklustre start to the season; and a week of mountain stages to rival anything in the Alps and Pyrenees. Today, for instance, the race finishes atop a ski station where the final three miles of ascent are on the sort of unmade roads scarcely seen in the Tour de France since the early 60s – setting the scene for a memorably gritty battle between the specialist climbers.

But you will hunt in vain to find any trace of what the Giro has to offer in the sports pages (including in this paper). Is it merely a case of special pleading to ask whether the reams of copy devoted to, say, the playoff for Premiership promotion might be just a little myopic and insular?

Saturday July 23, 2005

Barring some monstrous accident, tomorrow's procession along the Champs Elysées will be less a bicycle race than a passing-out parade for its American winner, Lance Armstrong. At that point he will have sealed a very strong claim to be cycling's greatest-ever champion by winning the Tour de France for a seventh consecutive time. Only four other riders have won as many as five Tours: Anquetil, Merckx, Hinault and Indurain. Seven straight wins is a record unlikely ever to be equalled.

The day also marks his retirement. For the consummate sports professional, whose preparation is never less than meticulous and whose training regime is famously punishing, it seems appropriate that Armstrong should crown his career by going out so emphatically at the top of his game. Those rivals who still have a season or two left in their legs will heave a sigh of relief.

The statistics of sporting success are one thing, but what Armstrong has brought to cycling transcends the special interest of any given sport. Lance is, above all, a great story. The son of an impoverished single mother, he triumphed to get a foothold in a notoriously tough sport, became one of its youngest-ever world champions – and then faced a cancer that threatened to end not just his career but his life.

And then the comeback to end all comebacks: he returned from surgery and chemotherapy, his very physiology and psychology seemingly reconstructed by his near-death experience, to win one of the most extreme tests of fitness and endurance in sport. And not once, but five, six, seven times.

Even the timing of his back-from-the-dead feat was perfect. In 1998 the Tour de France had suffered the worst doping scandal of its history when a team helper was caught with a boot-load of illegal drugs on the eve of the race. With people wondering whether there was a single clean rider left in the professional peloton, the Tour desperately needed to recover its prestige. Armstrong's 1999 win could not have come at a better time.

Many since have questioned whether his remarkable transformation from an unfulfilled young talent to the post-cancer world-beater that he has become could have been achieved without artificial stimulants. But Armstrong has never tested positive and sues anyone who calls him a cheat. He is as unrelenting and aggressive in defending his reputation as he is in riding his bike.

And that reputation has been considerably enhanced by the bestselling books about his life. The first and best, It's Not About the Bike, turned a minority-sport athlete into an inspirational cancer survivor in the eyes of the public. Since then Lance's Livestrong campaign has given the world a new fashion item – the charity wristband.

It may be impossible not to admire Lance, but it is hard to warm to him. His chiselled features are due to a very low body-fat ratio, but they speak also of an armoured flawlessness, a calculating ruthlessness. That, with his apparent physical invulnerability and virtually superhuman performance, suggest something of the replicant or android: is he human, is he real, or some kind of bionic man?

His perfect career admits no error or blemish. He seems now to ride less a bicycle than a seamless conveyor belt to stardom.

So what next? There is speculation that, back home, he may run for governor. Minnesota had an ex-wrestler, California has a former bodybuilder, so why not a one-time racing cyclist for Texas? At least, it is noted, he would be more liberal than some former governors of the state: Armstrong has criticised the invasion of Iraq, and his partner, the singer Sheryl Crow, is positively right on. The only authorised version, however, is that he is looking forward to spending more time with his kids. Of course. Perfect.

And what of his legacy? It is hard to imagine any rider ever exercising such a single-minded domination of the sport. Arguably, it will be good for the Tour de France that Lance is retiring. Mere mortals will have a chance to compete and win. It will be a race, rather than a kind of rolling roadshow of one man's supremacy.

At the same time, Armstrong's retirement will leave a vast and gaping vacuum: a sense that whatever follows will somehow be smaller, diminished. For once, the sports cliche about "the end of an era" is apt. I fancy that those watching on Sunday afternoon as Lance crosses the line for the last time will have a ghostly apprehension of a banner reading "The End" and, in their mind's eye, the credits will begin to roll. Already the idea of the Tour without Lance feels like an epic without a hero. The real question is not whether cycling will ever again produce such a great champion, but whether it will ever again have such a great story.

from Rapha (www.rapha.cc), Autumn 2006

THE NEARLY-PERFORMANCE

Which, in any given season, is the race that sticks in the memory? If you win one, it might be that. But often those are a blur, the sharpness of your recall somehow smudged and swamped by the euphoria of crossing the line first. And then you will be haunted by the faint but unavoidable suspicion that if you managed to win it, then it must have been just ever so slightly too easy: you got lucky, perhaps, or the field was underpowered.

There are many races in between, edited into a nondescript mental showreel of long suffering and short highlights. Ultimately forgettable stuff you wouldn't trouble your best friend with the telling of. No, there's just one kind of race that sticks and stays in the mind, inscribing itself with a lasting significance like acid eating out the marks on an etching plate. And that is the race of disappointment, the nearly-performance that ended in failure, the great effort ventured in vain.

You know the scenario from the first week of the Tour: the day-long break swept up by the sprinters within sight of the line. The way that the escapists, almost always pros you've never heard of or hear of again, disappear into the swarming peloton expresses it perfectly: they dared to aspire; their return to anonymity is complete. These journeymen worked all day, toiling under the sun, sweating and hurting, feeling their strength ebb, but knowing there was no option but utter commitment and a prayer that the sprinters' teams might have miscalculated the gap on the run-in. When you feel sorry for them, you feel sorry for yourself – and every other dreamer-loser there's ever been. So, my memory. An undulating circuit in Essex, two hours up the A12 out of London. A field full of first cats chasing late-season points; everyone with the same agenda, everyone fit enough to follow wheels all day. Only a fool would think that the winning break would go on the first lap. That left five more laps, of 11 miles each.

But it's not when, but who, I tell myself. This is a promising group: two strong juniors, three solid seniors. Five, a good number to work together. The rhythm is steady, through and off: you get into that zone where you're working just below the threshold of real pain. It's constant labour, but not impossible. Often you feel better when you're on the front, riding at your own tempo. I try to resist the temptation to do long turns. Roll through, turn a few revs, swing off. There's plenty to concentrate on, following wheels tidily, staying out of the wind.

After two more laps, though, the momentum is imperceptibly but surely slackening. The chase behind is in full cry. Two more, now three, riders join us. The peloton is just seconds behind. Up the one short, sharp rise in the circuit a mile and a quarter from the finish, our group is almost caught. It's touch and go – whether to sit up and accept the inevitable, or to press on and hope the gap goes out again on the descent.

It does. And looking around the new group, I begin to take heart. There are enough teams here to encourage the hope that the chase behind will be disorganised. Half a lap later, a time check from the motorbike gives us 30 seconds. We toil on. I make myself eat and drink. I know my body needs it, even if the starchy-sweet sports drink and fruit bars seem scarcely edible. We roll through, but now and again people are missing turns. All of us are hurting; some of us are struggling. The road starts to seem lumpier and rougher. The morning mist is clearing, but in its place comes a breeze that always seems a cross-headwind wherever we are on the circuit.

Up the climb again, and the break is losing coherence. When we turn a corner into the headwind soon after, the Heronsport guy in pale-blue jersey launches an attack. My first thought is: this is still too far out, almost three laps to go. My second thought is: the break's not working anyway; better to be in the better half of it. I counter quickly to get his wheel before the gap gets too great. Behind us, not much reaction. I rest for a few seconds on Heronsport's wheel, then pull through. The die is cast: this is the new move.

Just one other rider bridges, the lanky Glendene junior. Heronsport has a team-mate behind, and now so does Glendene. That leaves only three riders who will chase.

The calculation is correct. Glendene comes up to us and rides straight through to take a long turn. An ominous sign. Within two or three miles, the split is consolidated; the rest of the original break is not coming back. We are it, the head of affairs.

But now, the truth. This pace is killing me. I know I have to do my turn, but with just two partners, it is hard even to grab a wheel. You have just seconds in the slipstream desperately trying to recover before you have to pull again. We've already been out in front for nearly 40 miles, and I'm bouncing off the redline. At this moment, the effort is so intense that everything else starts to shut down; you don't see or hear things you normally would. It's a dangerous time because your handling skills and concentration fail. It's the moment in the race when people touch wheels or even ride right off the road into the gutter, seeing stars.

Heronsport is suffering too, but Glendene just seems to get stronger, as if he is sucking up our pain and thriving on it. Whereas I'm now constantly fishing for a ratio that won't break my legs, he doesn't touch his gears. He just sits there, rock solid, grinding away relentlessly in the 12 sprocket, regardless of the road's shifting gradients.

Penultimate time up the climb, Heronsport lets go. Glendene and I look round: should we let him get back on, give him a chance to recover and start working again? No. He's toast. He can hardly keep his bike rolling. No time for sentiment: press on. Hesitate and it's over.

Glendene makes the pace again. I try to come through, but the road seems horribly pitted and heavy. Every tiny rise murders me. I become all too aware that when I'm on the front, we are going more slowly. Too slowly. Another time check: 25 seconds, and still more than half a lap to go. While Heronsport was still there, I could bluff that I wasn't the strongest but I wasn't the weakest either. Now there's no one to fool, least of all myself. All I can achieve is to try to hold Glendene's wheel and get to the finish in one piece. I ask his permission; he assents. Once resolved, I take heart. How hard can that be, to sit behind someone and follow their wheel home?

I have my answer within a mile or two. Soon, nothing is working. Glendene is still churning that 12 cog, and the only thing keeping me on his wheel is willpower. I know that if I lose it by a yard, I'm finished: on my own, I wouldn't be able to ride at more than 16mph now. The bunch is closing at 25.

We reach the point where the break first went, 50 miles and 5 laps earlier: a series of innocuous bends in a country road, just occasionally creeping upwards in a false flat. Suddenly, I've lost Glendene's wheel. For a few seconds, he hovers tantalisingly within seeming reach. I try to get out of the saddle to jump across, but nothing happens. My legs have gone. Three miles to go, and all I had to do was stay on his wheel to collect a solid second place. Now nothing. Before, on the start sheet, I was somebody; here, I'm no one.

I sit up and recover for a few seconds. Then, round the last bend behind me, comes the front of the bunch. I'm so blown, I'm not sure if I can even get back in the main group. Glendene has perhaps 15 seconds; he's within sight of the bunch when the road straightens. For me, it's over. I don't even remember how I got up the final climb, but somehow I clung to the remnants. The main group is now stretched out on the descent, the front of the pack scenting blood, jockeying for position in the sprint, hunting down each new attack. How can Glendene possibly stay away from this hungry, roiling mass?

At three hundred yards, I am far enough behind to have some elevation and see the finish, almost dispassionately. I can make out Glendene's arms flying up in victory as he crosses the line – just two, maybe three, seconds ahead of the flailing sprinters.

What a ride, to force his breakaway partners off his wheel without even attacking them, and then stay clear of the final charge. A win in the grand style.

I wonder if he'll remember it always.

SIX

RIDE ON: THE ETHICAL BICYCLE RIDER

Latterly, the home of the Two Wheels column has been in the Ethical Living section of Thursday's G2 (the Guardian's features supplement), which is half an explanation for the title of this chapter. But not the whole of it.

One of the curious things about being a cyclist, and a pretty devoted one for more than 20 years of adult life, is that cycling has moved from being a private eccentricity to, practically, a public moral imperative. Riding a bike these days is part of doing one's bit to save the planet. There were those of us who always thought, of course, that cyclists were on the side of the angels, but it's good to know for sure. Then again, cycling's new-found place in the "good life" carries with it a duty not just to congratulate ourselves on being godly in our greenliness, but also to consider how perhaps we fall short.

The fact that cycling has become part of the environmentally correct lifestyle movement raises all sorts of complex and interesting questions – what old post-Marxists such as I used to term, sagely, as "contradictions" (that is, an inconveniently irreconcilable collision between theory and reality). As I am a fraud compared with my colleague, and king of ethical living, Leo Hickman, when it comes to assessing the carbon footprint of, say, a new aluminium bike (which will have used probably several gigawatts in the smelting thereof) and a new carbon one (manufactured, after all, from petroleum-based materials), these pieces mainly amount to thinking aloud about the issues, rather than providing any comprehensive audit.

And then, besides the eco-cycling stuff, there was my brief, unhappy foray into the ethicist's realm: to ride with iPod or not to ride with iPod? Here, all I succeed in proving is that I am a connoisseur not only of "contradictions", but of self-contradictions too. Clearly, if cycling needs an agony uncle or aunt of real moral authority, I'm not it.

Wednesday October 11, 2006

I was struck by an advert in the weekend papers for BP's "targetneutral" scheme (targetneutral.com). The concept is that you, as a motorist, make a voluntary donation proportionate to the carbon cost of your driving that will fund renewable energy projects. It's a cute idea, so I had to try it.

I have a Volvo estate (yep, we're talking family-guy stereotypes here), which I use as little as possible but which is in the top-rate of VED tax for CO_2 emissions. Using the site's calculator, I find I put out about 2.7 tonnes of CO_2 a year, which targetneutral.com says I can offset by a £15 gift to the cause. As it costs at least £60 to fill a tank, I'd say this is pretty much a bargain for a year's conscience-clear motoring.

Except that I can't help feeling it's a completely token measure. In his new book, Heat, George Monbiot calculates that in order to stabilise climate change short of catastrophe, we need a 90% cut in carbon emissions by 2030. That means we'd all have an allowance of 0.33 tonnes of CO_2 a year. With my Volvo, I've spent the entire family carbon allowance twice over before even switching on a light.

In fact, I spend more than the family's carbon allowance on the precious Volvo. Like all cars, it's a money pit. Insurance premiums, parking costs, petrol, servicing ... it tots up to thousands a year. Just on economic grounds, it's unsustainable. And we live near the city centre, so we don't even have the suburbanites' excuse that there's no other way to get around.

If you stop to think rationally for even a minute, it's blindingly obvious that cars – and driving as we know it – simply do not belong to the future. The veteran thinktanker Mayer Hillman, who has recently been working in the area of "personal carbon budgeting", puts it baldly in the current issue of London Cyclist magazine: we simply have to get used to the idea of travelling less. The right to drive everywhere leads straight up the dead end of climate-change disaster.

But the difficulty we have is being able to imagine a car-less future. Everything is telling me to ditch mine: the planet would be better-off, and so would I. What's stopping me? It's not as if driving is fun anymore: mostly, I'm stuck in traffic, breathing in fumes and fuming myself. Part of me is scared about how irrevocable the decision is: once out of the car market, it's ruinous to get back in. But much of it, I suspect, is emotional. I've grown up with the idea that being a fully fledged adult (especially a male one) is synonymous with car ownership. I'm proud to be a bike person, but am I ready not to be a car person?

Actually, that really is pathetic. A third-hand Volvo, anyone?

Wednesday June 21, 2006

The weekend saw tens of thousands taking to their bikes for the British Heart Foundation London to Brighton ride; now we're in the middle of Bike Week. Last week, the Independent newspaper ran a whole week of pro-bike features. All reasons to be cheerful about cycling; it feels as though the tide has finally turned our way.

But how much difference does our hard-won progress make to the big picture? The irony about the UK's bike revival is that roughly 60% of the new bicycles we buy (about 4.5m a year) are made in China – even while the Chinese are deserting theirs in droves.

Irony number two is that most Chinese people could not afford the bikes they are making for us. While we get wonderful light alloy machines, they are still stuck with the venerable Flying Pigeon, which weighs twice as much. At 240 yuan (£16), the People's bicycle still represents a substantial outlay for China's rural poor. Then again, it does have reinforced tubing so that it can carry a pig.

Cycle use has doubled in London over the past five years, but in Beijing bike use is falling off a cliff. In 1998, 60% of commuters rode to work; by 2002, it was down to 20%. With more than 1,000 cars being added to Beijing's streets every day, you don't need to be an expert analyst to see which way the trend is travelling.

China has a huge circle to square. What Margaret Thatcher here once dubbed – in an oddly Maoist turn of phrase – "the great car economy" is a vital driver of growth: motor manufacturing is regarded as a "pillar industry" by China's communist leaders. But its cities are already choking in smog and clogged with traffic. It took Britain four or five decades of growing car ownership and declining cycle use to realise that that model was ultimately unsustainable. And we've only just begun to pull the policy levers to reverse it.

Persuading people to change their habits is a fantastically intensive process. The "personal travel plan" is the new buzz phrase among transport wonks: it means knocking on thousands of doors and talking to people about why they might like to try cycling. In the People's Republic, such elaborate measures are not required: people tend to do as they're told. The Chinese are not yet being ordered back on to their bikes, but one small ray of light is that last week an official in the Construction Ministry announced that bike lanes were being restored.

It is too early for optimism, however. The chairman of the China Bicycle Association, Wang Fenghe, recently insisted China would remain a "kingdom of bicycles". Yet Wang himself has given up cycling. He was knocked off his bike by a car.

Wednesday December 7, 2005

Like most cyclists, I suspect, I float around on my bike buoyed up by the idea that I am doing my bit to save the planet. Compared with motorists, of course, this is mostly true. For each passenger kilometre, cars put out 200-300 grammes of carbon dioxide (the chief greenhouse gas). Cyclists, meanwhile, are rated at zero – which may not be quite realistic, given that we are breathing as we ride, but our CO_2 emissions are negligible.

So far so good, but what about the bikes we ride? Here the picture gets murkier. I rang Chris Juden, the Cyclists' Touring Club's technical officer and an authority in the field.

The bad news is that bikes are getting less green. The old

steel frames were heavy but it was standard to get a lifetime guarantee. Today, lighter bikes have built-in obsolescence: aluminium frames fatigue, and carbon-fibre parts (such as forks) bear stickers recommending replacement after just three years.

Even maintenance has been affected by the demise of the very idea of the "consumer durable". "The cost of labour to service is higher," explains Juden, "so it's no longer worth manufacturing parts in such a way that they can be repaired." So bike bits are actually designed to be disposable.

And then there's the air (and sea and road) miles issue. Like everything else, the bike industry is global. Juden estimates that, in the sum of their parts, most modern bikes will have already travelled further on their way to the shop than they are ever likely to be pedalled. And let's not even get into labour condi-tions and environmental regulation in China and Vietnam.

What's the answer? Well, the nearest thing to a fair-trade, organic, ethically correct bicycle is to buy local – either a British-made brand such as Brompton, or a steel lightweight from an artisan frame-builder. Then the longer you have it and the further you go, the more marginal its original environmen-tal cost becomes.

In other words, all you need to do is keep riding it.

Wednesday February 15, 2006

My favourite cycling jacket has a beautiful design feature. One of the back pockets has a buttonhole on the inside, and then there are two little loops on the hem around the armhole. The idea is that you could have an MP3 player stowed in your rear pocket with the headphone wires routed up inside your jacket. It's a nicely executed, clever detail. But one I'll never use.

On Monday, a coroner's court in London heard the beginning of an inquest into the death of Patricia McMillan. The 32-year-old law student was cycling to work when she was hit by a lorry, dragged under its wheels and killed. She was wearing an iPod at the time, and a close friend speculated whether her failure to hear the lorry had contributed to the fatal incident.

Although this explanation remains, at this point, speculative (pending the coroner's full findings), it hasn't prevented newspapers reporting the iPod factor as a cautionary tale. There are two annoying subtexts here – one implicitly blaming the victim of the tragedy, and the other reinforcing the idea that the Grim Reaper waits on every corner to scythe down cyclists – but I'm trying to get past that. The heart of the matter, surely, is this: just how dangerous is it to listen to music while you ride?

The idea is very appealing. But I don't do it because, instinctively, I feel I need all my senses to be safe. You're always listening for the car behind, even if you're barely conscious of doing so. And often it's precisely because you're listening out that you look behind, and then reassure yourself that the driver has seen you.

There's no way of knowing whether being able to hear the lorry would have saved McMillan. But what cyclists do know, because it happens every day, is that pedestrians step out in front of us because they haven't heard us coming. This problem is only made worse by people who are on the phone or have earphones in.

But perhaps there's a philosophical as well as a practical reason for cyclists to avoid turning ourselves into dangerously distracted solipsists on wheels. The iPod phenomenon belongs to a new existential mode in which we do all we can to insulate ourselves from our environment in a capsule of creature comforts. Every individual becomes his or her own gated community: status-conscious, exclusive and forbidding uninvited intrusion. The car, with its sound system, climate control and cupholders, is the apotheosis of this antisocial protective shield. I like to think that the bicycle offers, among other things, a different way of being in the world, one that is potentially more human and social. And like music itself, the best way to enjoy cycling is live and unplugged.

Wednesday July 26, 2006

I'm about to execute a U-turn. The rule for making such a manoeuvre, of course, is that you look over your shoulder carefully. In this case, however, I suspect no precaution will prevent me from being run over by a juggernaut of angry correspondents.

It was a few months ago, sadly in the wake of a young woman having been knocked off her bike and killed, that I wrote about listening to music while riding. The media had seized on the unhelpful speculation – even as the inquest was adjourned – of a "friend" of the unfortunate woman that listening to her iPod may have been a contributory factor.

The dangers of iPod-listening while cycling is a favourite theme of mid-market newspapers, for whom it is so perfect a cautionary tale it might have been penned by Hilaire Belloc ("Dorothy, Who Listened to her iPod whilst Bicycling, and was Squashed by a Motorcar"). It is true that the Royal Society for the Prevention of Accidents cautiously advises against cycling while "distracted by music", but surely a double standard is being applied: when did we read a story about the menace of music-listening motorists?

But to get to my U-turn: I didn't come down against iPod-listening because it's dangerous. The jury is still out on that. The two conclusions I draw from my experience are, first, that you do not lose all your ambient hearing, and second, that you can compensate for any hearing deficit by extra visual checks. Instinct tells me that I am marginally increasing the risk by listening to music, but that it is within my power to adjust for that.

I came out against iPod-listening because, I said, it cuts you off from fully being in the world. In retrospect, this argument strikes me as flaky and specious – not least because a lot of my cycling is a solipsistic activity anyway.

But the real reason for my U-turn came last week as I arrived at work. I was riding behind a colleague: we both made beautiful hand signals when we turned into a sidestreet, and again as we wheeled into the cul-de-sac behind the office. As we locked our bikes (and I took out my earphones), she asked: "Did you hear that cab driver?" "No, what did he say?" "'You should have to pay road tax!'" Just because we had slowed him down momentarily – despite our exemplary road manners.

If I had heard such stupid abuse, I would almost certainly have got into a fruitless shouting match, with the result that I would have spent the next hour at my desk trying to quell my adrenalised rage. Frankly, it made my day that I'd been listening to Keith Jarrett instead.

Wednesday October 4, 2006

This week, David Cameron's green taskforce adviser, Zac Goldsmith, told the Conservative party conference that, instead of taxing "good things" (such as trust funds), it was time to start taxing "bad things like pollution". I couldn't agree more

– and I'm sure the editor of The Ecologist magazine would concur with me that when it comes to pollution on our roads, mopeds and motorbikes are very bad things.

No? Dear me. It seems Goldsmith is often seen doing the rounds from his house to the offices of The Ecologist, and visiting friends and family, all in and around Chelsea, not on a bicycle but on a black Vespa. Somehow, then, it must have escaped his notice that, for each passenger kilometre, powered two wheelers (PTWs, in the jargon) produce about six times as much methane and carbon monoxide, seven times as many particulates, and a whopping 11 times as much benzene as cars do. What's more, even though their engines are smaller, the crude two-stroke engines of mopeds are more polluting than the four-stroke ones of motorbikes. So if pollution is a bad thing we should charge for, Zac, then that Vespa really ought to be – as his fellow Tory conference speaker Jeanette Winterson so charmingly put it – "taxed up the arse".

Why am I so exercised about scooters all of a sudden? It is not so sudden, really. With growing congestion, more and more people seem to be using these infernal machines. To begin with, I thought to myself, let's be tolerant – they're also on two wheels, after all. As relatively vulnerable road users, like cyclists, perhaps there is some common cause to be made. Now I realise this was terribly naive: scooters are simply a public nuisance.

And it is not just the fact that they make clouds of choking blue smoke that I have to breathe in. Their owners must number among the most inconsiderate and irresponsible drivers on the road. They make red-light-running, pavement-riding cyclists look like pillars of the community.

I exclude motorcyclists from this charge because they have to undertake training and testing, whereas anyone with a car driving licence can hop on a moped. This presumably explains why so many of them seem to think they are entitled to drive in cycle lanes and weave in and out of traffic like maniacs (because no one has specifically told them not to). The greater premium there is on road space, the more mopeds compete with cyclists: they want to use the same bit of road that we do. And the problem is that they think they can ride like cyclists, with no sense of consequence from the fact that they are bigger, heavier and faster (as well as infinitely noisier and dirtier).

Taxing? Very. In short, the moped is the best argument ever mounted for making the polluter pay.

SEVEN

ZEN AND THE ART: BICYCLE CULTURE AND CYCLING SUBCULTURES

Is there such a thing as cycling culture? Riding in tandem with the spirit of modernism, cycling has inspired hundreds of artists, writers, filmmakers and musicians – from Pablo Picasso to Iris Murdoch, and from Steven Spielberg to Kraftwerk – who have incorporated and celebrated the bicycle in their work. It would be easy to curate an exhibition of the art of cycling, for example – or rather, of art in which cycling features. Far fewer artists can be said to have made the bicycle truly their subject. In the same way that, with the exception of a few great books on cycling, "cycling literature" consists chiefly of an anthology of "mentions" of cycling by notable authors.

So, the notion of cycling culture as a unified project might be hard to sustain, but that's not to belittle the pleasures and insights to be had from the anthologising impulse. It is enriching to discover these apercus, commentaries and adaptations. It is impossible, I believe, to know Picasso's Bull's Head and not, in some sense, to see it whenever your eye falls on the curved drop of a racing bike's handlebars. Your perception has been altered by his vision – and perhaps that moment of communion is the truest instance of "bicycle culture".

An academic debate, possibly, but what cycling definitely has, in abundance, are subcultures. At its more extreme, cycling has generated a series of tight-knit tribes bound together by shared values and interests and by the practice of certain rituals. Cycling clubs alone could generate material for a phalanx of PhD-seeking anthropologists, and that's before you get into the more obscure racing fraternities. But anyone can be a participant-observer in the various worlds that cyclists make for themselves by their passionate involvement with their bicycles and their association with one another.

Often, you find yourself inside one of these worlds before you know it, like Alice falling down the white rabbit's burrow. The trick then is to see it anew, as strange as it undoubtedly is, but still with empathy. The value of understanding these cycling subcultures is the unexpected recognition of yourself in others. Which, at bottom, is a fancy way of saying cycling makes us friends.

Wednesday March 15, 2006

If you go for a recreational ride at the weekend, every cyclist you meet coming the other way will give you a little wave or a nod. Get a puncture on some country road and, like as not, a passing rider will stop to check you have everything you need to get home. And when you break your ride for a tea stop, the other cyclists in the cafe will greet you with pleasantries about the cold, the wind, the hills and which is the best cake to choose.

I'm the first to wax romantic about "the fellowship of the road". There is a tremendous sense of solidarity in every cyclist based on the shared experience of a passion. It is the instinctive empathy of identification you get when you feel you belong to a community. You can ride the world over and find it wherever you go.

But we're a rum lot, too. For all I know, the rider I pull up next to at the traffic lights on a Monday morning may be the guy who saluted me on Sunday, but do we acknowledge each other? Do we heck. There's certainly no nodding or waving, let alone chatting. Instead, we each pretend the other doesn't exist.

I've tried telling myself that this is just another instance of that very English etiquette about respecting people's preferred illusion – on any form of transport – that they are in a bubble of privacy and solitary contemplation: the way everyone on the underground carriage acts as if they're the only person there, even when they may be in enforced bodily contact with strangers. But this doesn't seem to fit the cycling subculture: we're not forced into the same confined space; we are each masters of our own conveyance, autonomous and free.

So why aren't we more friendly? In an experimental spirit, I have sometimes tried breaking the ice with a sardonic remark addressed to the rider next to me about something we've both just witnessed. Occasionally you get treated as a marginal loony, space invader or suspect sexual harasser, but mostly people seem only too glad to respond in kind. In fact, I think they feel, as I do, almost relieved that the tension inherent in these artificial-ignoring scenarios has been broken for once.

It's not just that we're English; it's something specific to cyclists. For all that we ride together sometimes, we don't run with the herd. There is a bit of the loner about us, the cat that walks by itself. And sometimes, we hiss and scratch – even at our own kind. In the past week or so, for things I've written, other cyclists have called me a bully, an arse and a middle-class social-ist from north London. (That last really stung: I live in south London, dammit.)

But would I have it any other way? No. And I will defend to the death your right to ignore me at the lights.

Wednesday September 7, 2005

How else could one possibly go to London's first Bicycle Film Festival than by bike?

I wasn't the only one. By 7pm last Saturday the stands and railings outside the Cochrane Theatre, next to Central St Martin's College in Holborn, were chock-full with bicycles. But, apparently, this particular location is notorious for bike theft. So it wasn't very reassuring that one of the first films up that evening was a short called Bike Thief.

In a four-minute movie, Casey Neistat (half of the multime-dia artist duo the Neistat brothers, best known for their "iPod's Dirty Secret" campaign) steals his own bike four times from streets in New York. Hilariously, he even uses an angle-grinder to cut the lock without his seemingly nefarious activity provok-ing the slightest interest from passersby.

The Bicycle Film Festival is new to London, but not to the world. Its director, Brendt Barbur, a lean thirtysomething with a mane of dark brown hair and short beard, wearing jeans and yellow festival T-shirt, founded it in 2001. A native of north California, he had moved from San Francisco to New York, where he was seriously injured after being hit by a bus on his bike. The incident left him determined to do something posi-tive to highlight the plight of cyclists.

The festival has grown each year in New York and San

Francisco. To begin with, Barbur was ransacking the archives for cycling cinema classics, but as the festival gained momentum, it has attracted more and more new submissions. This year, Barbur was choosing from 350, mostly short, films by ambitious young videographers with a biking passion. Friday evening's screening featured an astonishing five-minute piece by Lucas Brunelle, Monster Track VI – a homage to New York's most skilled messengers that has you flinching in your seat as a camera follows them on a helter-skelter run through the city.

The festival's *pièce de résistance* was a 40-minute documentary about the NYPD's crackdown on the Critical Mass movement – the now global "happening" on the last Friday of every month in which cyclists congregate in their hundreds and thousands to convoy through the city for a celebratory couple of hours – ever since last year's Republican National Convention. Judging by the numbers who stayed for a Q&A with the co-directors, Elizabeth Press and Andrew Lynn, Barbur's brand of bicycle evangelism found a sympathetic audience on its first London outing. Best of all, my bike was still there when I left.

Thursday April 19, 2007

From HG Wells to Henry Miller, cycling has produced some great writing – although it must be admitted that it has also produced plenty of dross, from HG Wells to Henry Miller. The bike has inspired numerous artists, too: Marcel Duchamp, Fernand Léger and Joseph Beuys, to name but a few who have incorporated or represented the bicycle in their work. Somehow, cycling combines an ordinary, everyday object with

an intense individual experience and an aesthetics of performance in a way that, from the birth of modernism, has moved
creative spirits.

But what can we say about cycling on celluloid? This is not
such a rich seam. We can think of memorable scenes: the idyllic
bicycling interlude in Butch Cassidy and the Sundance Kid, or
ET's memorable moonlit ride. And plenty of incidental
moments where bikes are props, as in Some Like It Hot. We can
even think of films where bicycles or cycling form the premise
or locale of the film, as in Vittorio de Sica's Bicycle Thieves and
Saturday Night and Sunday Morning, the adaptation of Alan
Sillitoe's novel set around the Raleigh factory in Nottingham.

But when you think of how the car, in cinema history, has
spawned an entire genre – the road movie – cycling is clearly the
poor relation. The reasons are not hard to perceive: the golden
age of Hollywood studios in the 1940s and 1950s coincided in
time and place precisely with the first great era of the automo-
bile: LA was a city built on the glamorous prosperity of movies
and motoring. And then there was the technology of filming:
big, heavy cameras could be mounted on trucks to get good
footage of driving – think of that movie-born sub-genre, the car
chase – but was less well suited to capturing the more delicate,
subjective experience of cycling. (I think today's minute digital
helmet-cams are about to revolutionise the way we see the
cyclist's eye-view, but that's another story.)

The honourable exceptions to the rule that cycling has not
translated well to the big screen are few and far between. Peter
Yates's Breaking Away, which won an Oscar for best screenplay
in 1980, is a charming coming-of-age study of life in a provin-
cial college town in the US, in which one of the principal
characters is a young man obsessed with all things cycling and

Italian. But the cycle-racing follow-up feature from its author, Steve Tesich, was American Flyers, which even Kevin Costner's mum would have to admit was a bike-crash of a movie.

Perhaps we can make another exception, though, for a contemporary home-grown effort: The Flying Scotsman, a film adaptation of Graeme Obree's book about his battle to win the world hour record and his parallel struggle with depression. The film premiered at Edinburgh last year, but opens just in time for this year's Tour de France on July 6. As human drama, it's not the deepest or most rewarding – but then that may be too much to expect: almost by definition, great athletes are single-minded and not of many dimensions. But Obree's story is told with a type of earnest commitment by director and actors, which you feel is authentic and of a piece with its subject. During shooting, Obree himself rode the bike-cam behind Jonny Lee Miller for the velodrome scenes. Somehow, for one of the great pursuit riders of all time, that seems very appropriate.

Wednesday September 20, 2006

To the uninitiated, the world of the club cyclist must seem pretty weird and forbidding. It sometimes still feels that way when you are one. Look at what it involves: odd clothes, strange rituals at unsociable hours, greeting fellow members in public with discreet flicks of the hand ... it makes Freemasonry seem socially inclusive.

Suppose you've become a keen cyclist and want to find like-minded people to ride with. How would you even know where to start finding a club? A quest such as this can seem an arcane pursuit within one that is arcane enough already.

There's something very British about the inaccessibility and "unto-itself-ness" of the cycling club. So much signposting in this country is inadequate for the same reason: you are just supposed to know where to go – or, says the subtext of the non-existent directions, you have no business going there at all.

It's more shyness than unfriendliness, perhaps, but even when we join a club or society, we seem to do so ambivalently. I was struck, recently, with the contrast when I joined a Sunday "club run" in France. As each rider arrived before the start, he (it was "he" exclusively, I'm afraid) would shake the hand of every person there – a scene no doubt repeated in every small town in France. That would never happen here. A nod and a murmur suffices, thank you.

There is one way that British cycling club culture improves on the French: at least our jerseys aren't cluttered with ads for the local supermarket or garage. We can't get the sponsorship.

Possibly I exaggerate. And perhaps I describe a world now disappeared. Several of the clubs I grew up with just 20 years ago are virtually defunct. The ones that have survived have had to find ways of turning themselves outwards and recruiting new members. My old club, the Velo Club de Londres (many British cycling clubs are prefixed "VC", consciously following the French example) does a fine job coaching young people at Herne Hill velodrome in south London, and has also cultivated some of the best women racers in the country.

Another local club, the Dulwich Paragon, has gone a different route, away from sport, finding new members by organising easier, social rides. These have the additional merit of starting and finishing at the Cafe St Germain, atop Crystal Palace, where you can taste the best croissants this side of Calais. Or Croydon, certainly. Like others, the Paragon has also got into running charity rides and cyclo-sportives, such as the Ride of the Falling Leaves the weekend after next.

But some things never change. Go on a club run today and you will still encounter some old boy who'll tell you that you are doing it all wrong. That would be me.

Thursday November 23, 2006

So I was sitting in the back row at the concert, waiting for the interval to finish and the music to start again. Because it was a Thursday, I had that week's copy of Cycling Weekly. CW – or "the comic", as it is disrespectfully but affectionately known – is an institution for club cyclists. They like to grumble about it, but everyone reads it.

What's in it? Well, at the front runs a digest of news from the continental pro scene, a round-up of domestic road racing, and general news; then interviews with leading riders, features on nutrition and training, product tests, results and classifieds. It takes about 20 minutes to read from cover to cover. My wife derides it as my "bike porn". Each week, I devour it like candy.

This week I had been too rushed to look at it in the morning, so had stashed it in my bike bag, thinking ahead to the gig I was going to – sadly alone – that evening. I was settling in to my furtive five-minute session with CW when a guy took his seat next to me. I saw him check out my reading, then unfold his own magazine: Cycle Sport (CW's more glossy monthly sibling). So, of course, we were off talking.

"What bike do you have?" That was a little forward as an icebreaker, I thought – bikes being very personal things – but he was young, still a teenager. I told him about my Colnago, because it's a name anyone who is interested in racing bikes will have heard of, and it usually impresses. But I was the one who was impressed when he told me his, acquired only months earlier, was a Gios. And not a modern Gios, but an old steel classic, trademarked by its gorgeous Italian-blue paint job. He flicked through his magazine and showed me a picture of the very model, being ridden by the great Belgian champion Roger de Vlaeminck, circa 1975. A collector's item.

But before I could discover how he came by it, the lights went down and the band came on. (The Esbjorn Svensson Trio, to whom our critic, John Fordham, gave a favourable notice.) I didn't mind sharing the music with my neighbour after that. Being a pianist, he knew more than me anyway. And he was happy to talk bikes afterwards, with all the enthusiasm of an initiate.

A happy coincidence. But how coincidental? In his fine book One More Kilometre and We're in the Showers, Tim Hilton notes the preponderance of writers, artists and musicians among cyclists. Which argues a certain aesthetic tendency. Then again, Hilton observes, you meet a lot of posties too; cycling is a sport that suits them because the shift work leaves plenty of time for training. So perhaps it's just that creative types cycle because they keep irregular hours and don't have money. After all, my friend and I were in the cheapest seats.

I prefer to think we found common interest because of our fine sensibilities.

Thursday December 7, 2006

When I turned up for my first Audax ride, about 20 years ago, in the car park of a pub somewhere near Maidenhead, the organisers of the ride – 100km hither and thither around the

Chiltern hills – looked askance at my bike. Didn't I know that I had to have mudguards? No, I didn't: otherwise, I suppose, I would have had them.

After considerable teeth-sucking and consultation, I was permitted to take part, but with the understanding that this was a once-only dispensation on account of my youth and ignorance; I could not expect such generous treatment again. Get some mudguards, lad.

Audax is an international organisation, with a British branch, that organises long-distance endurance events: "*randonnées*". These are not races – in fact, a maximum average speed of 30kph applies – but the idea is that a ride of 100km, 200km, or more, is completed within a given time. There are checkpoints on the course, where "*randonneurs*" must hand over their "*brevet*" cards – little carnets – to be stamped by an official to prove completion of each stage.

These are the ancient forerunners of today's more vogueish cyclo-sportives; and British cycling clubs run early-season events called reliability trials along similar lines. The most famous *randonnée* of all is the Paris-Brest-Paris (PBP to cognoscenti), a 1,200km, through-night-and-day marathon, which dates back to 1891 and is held every four years.

Audax has its own lore and adherents – a tough, often older, but gruffly warm breed. They usually ride touring bikes, of venerable steel construction, with well-worn Brooks saddles and old-fashioned black canvas Carradice saddlebags containing some kind of pre-Gore-Tex waterproof, woollen jersey, spare pair of socks and packet of fig rolls.

They will ride at the same steady lick, up hill and down dale, for hundreds of kilometres, apparently indefatigable and without complaint, in all weathers. It can be blowing a gale and they may be drenched by horizontal rain, but they will only complain if they have to ride behind someone without mudguards. Audax regulations still allow event organisers to specify mudguards as mandatory.

And, given recent weather, I've been reminded why. If you're riding close behind someone without mudguards, it can be hard to tell whether you are getting wetter from the rain or the spray off their tyres. Mostly, on the daily commute, there's no reason to cycle so close. Then one just marvels at the masochism of people who seem oblivious of the long damp stripe of rainwater, grit and road grime following the line of their spine from coccyx to neck. Very staining, too.

It's mysterious to me why anyone would endure a British winter without mudguards. Some may feel they spoil the look of their bike. Possibly, but not as much as the muck off the road does.

Teeth-sucking, you see: an essential cycling skill.

Wednesday May 17, 2006

People don't talk much about class and cycling. It's one of those things we all notice but are far too polite to mention. But the fact is there are two types of cyclist. One is white, middle-class, educated, and probably liberal in their politics; they have good-quality, new-ish bikes, with the right accessories. The other is either poor or teenaged, often non-white, and has whatever bike comes to hand – old and ill-maintained or cheap from Halfords.

This unspoken theme of class identity is often a subtext of confrontations between motorists and cyclists. Drivers are likely to be working-class; cyclists usually middle-class. Some of the simmering resentment that bubbles up when there's an incident is because motorists see us as snotty, posh and self-entitled. That's right: they're in the cars, we're on the bikes, but they're the ones with the inferiority complex. This is a huge reversal of where we were 50 or 60 years ago, when more than 10 million people still pedalled to work. But then, in the 1950s and 1960s, came postwar affluence and, as the Labour politician Tony Crosland once remarked, the middle classes could not pull the ladder of prosperity up after them: what his working-class constituents wanted were cars and foreign holidays. So, in the era of universal car ownership, riding a bike has become a largely middle-class lifestyle option.

None of this is said in a spirit of rancour or self-flagellation. But what got me thinking about this was a couple of pages from a new book by the veteran sustainable transport campaigner Lynn Sloman, Car Sick: Solutions for our Car-addicted Culture. Her explanation of the roots of cycling's revival makes fascinating reading. We tend to think the boom is due to more bike lanes, route maps and parking stands (with London, in particular, getting a boost from Ken Livingstone's congestion charge and commitment to cycling). Wrong, says Sloman: the recovery long predates the serious spending.

The London borough of Hackney led the way. According to census figures, just 2.5% of residents cycled to work in 1981; by 1991, this had risen to 4%; and in 2001, it stood at an amazing, almost Danish-style 7%. Partly this was "because the alternatives were so unattractive" – poor public transport and congestion. But "part of the explanation," she writes, "might also have been that the borough had a long history of radicalism, and started to attract young people who were environmentally aware and predisposed to cycling".

I know exactly who she means. The irony is delicious: the very same people – paid-up members of the progressive middle class – who were tarred with being "loony left" 20 years ago have now helped to make our cities more civilised. Thatcher's children? Ken's kids, more like.

from Rouleur, vol.4, 2007

BREAKING AWAY: AN ESSAY

Let me tell you my favourite scene from the movie.

Dave Stoller (Dennis Christopher) wears a yellow Campagnolo cap, with a red, white and green stripe. He sings arias from Italian opera when he's out training. He's even named his cat "Fellini". And he drives his father, a former stonecutter in Indiana's limestone quarries, crazy by calling him "Papa" and acting all "Eye-talian". Raymond doesn't understand what's happening to his son, and doesn't care to find out; he just knows he doesn't like it.

Raymond Stoller, a somewhat sour second-hand car salesman, played by Paul Dooley (a fine journeyman character actor who has never been out of work since the early 60s, and whom you've likely seen most recently as Larry David's father-in-law in Curb Your Enthusiasm), decides that he's had enough of his 19-year-old son Dave's affectations and that he's "going to have it out with him". Dave's offence – apart from being unable to make up his mind whether to get a job or go to college – is that he's obsessed with cycling and so, by extension, with all things Italian.

Watched by his wife (Barbara Barrie), we see Ray make for the bathroom where Dave has gone to take a shower after winning a bike race. But, instead of the expected confrontation, Ray returns to the corridor with an utterly stunned look on his face – the director, Peter York, evidently noticed Dooley's talent for expression, as the film closes with an affectionate freeze frame of him doing "astonishment" with heroic emphasis.

"He's shaving," Ray says flatly.

"Well? So what?" replies Dave's mother, Evelyn.

"His legs. He's shaving his legs."

A brief explanatory glimpse of Dave Stoller with one leg in the basin, shin lathered. And cut: no dwelling on the moment to milk the humour. No reaction from the mother; just on to the next scene. A good illustration, in fact, of why Breaking Away has been such a successful and enduring film since it premiered in 1979. That year, it was nominated for five Academy Awards, deservedly coming away in the end with the Oscar for best original screenplay, which had been written by a Yugoslavian emigre named Steve Tesich.

The story concerns four friends, fresh out of high school and kicking their heels for the summer in their hometown of Bloomington, Indiana, wondering that they will do next – which is to say, what they'll do with the rest of their lives. Their "leader" is Mike, played memorably by Dennis Quaid, with washboard stomach and pack of cigarettes tucked into the sleeve of his T-shirt, as a sort of pocket-sized version of Marlon Brando in On The Waterfront, who worries that his finest hour as the school's quarterback is behind him. He can see little future for himself in a town where jobs in the declining quarrying industry are scarce – other than getting into trouble with his older brother, a cop.

Together with Dave Stoller, the laidback, ironical Cyril (Daniel Stern) and "gutsy little guy" Moocher (Jackie Earle Haley) complete this quartet of "cutters", the derogatory nickname used by the snobbish upper-class college kids to describe

the "townies", the blue-collar sons and daughters of stonecut-
ters. The film's plot is driven along by this current of class
antagonism – first, as Dave falls for a college girl, Katherine
Bennett (Robyn Douglass), but stymies the romance by
pretending he's Italian, rather than reveal his more humble,
domestic roots; and then, as Mike persuades the gang to enter
the annual college students' bike race, the Little 500, as the
"Cutters" team, in an attempt to win back their pride and self-
respect after earlier humiliations at the hands of the privileged
varsity crowd.

Against the odds, they win, of course. And Dave goes to
college. Things don't work out with Katherine (just as well, or
the film might have dissolved in syrup), but you feel Dave
learned a lesson about life there: not only did he lose Katherine
because he pretended to be something he was not, but along
the way he lost his other romance, with all things Italian. In the
subplot of Dave's racing career, he finds himself in a break with
four riders from Team Cinzano, but discovers the world of
professional cycle-racing can be dirty and cruel when one of his
admired Italian co-escapists sticks his pump in Dave's front
wheel and ends his race with a clatter in the gutter. Disillusion,
you understand, is part of growing up.

Dave's redemption is that getting over his fear of failure and
of being ostracised by going to college leads to his meeting a
nice French girl on campus – and this time, he doesn't have to
come from anywhere other than home or be anything he isn't.
Only, his romantic openness to things European is what turns
his father Ray Stoller's neck in the film's final frame, when son
wishes father "Bonjour!" Mike's redemption is that winning the
Little 500 restores his dignity and confidence, and, you hope,
enables him to get past his embittered sense of inferiority.

Moocher is leaving town to work in Chicago, coincidentally as Katherine is (albeit in very different jobs, you imagine). Of Cyril, we know nothing: the last shot of him shows the tall, gangling youth in the midst of the Cutters team celebrations, yet somehow out of it.

A bittersweet coming-of-age comedy, Breaking Away is the sort of film you would describe as poignant. But what can be learned of its afterlife, especially of its Academy Award-winning writer, only makes it seem more so. It might appear ironic that a film about the struggle to grasp the American dream in heart-land midwest was written by someone born in what is now western Serbia, but the tension between idealised hopes and darker truths has perhaps always been seen and felt more keenly by the US's more recent immigrants.

For fans of cycling, Breaking Away has become iconic. As what might be termed "cycling films" go, the genre chiefly comprises documentary, with an excellent few, and many mediocre, at that. Decent dramas featuring cycling are practi-cally non-existent. Sad to say, a follow-up script of Tesich's, made in 1985 as American Flyers, and rather improbably star-ring Kevin Costner, was a turkey – practically a cautionary tale to counsel writers and directors trying to mix heroics of athletic endeavour with emotionally satisfying drama. Who can forget, without wincing, the burly, bearded Soviet rider who acted as the villain of the piece?

As caustic but spot-on as ever, the New Yorker's film critic, Pauline Kael – on Tesich's other major 1985 credit, as author of the screen adaptation of Nicholas Gage's story of his mother's self-sacrifice in civil war-era Greece, Eleni – said: "The job of writing the script was entrusted to the Yugoslavian-born Steve Tesich, who showed a lot of cocky humor in Breaking Away but has since brought a delirious, flag-waving Americanism and/or clanging anti-Communism to such projects as Eyewitness, Four Friends, and American Flyers. His contribution here is as disastrous as it was to those movies." Whatever the flaws of those films, you have to hope Tesich never read those lines, but it seems unlikely he did not.

Eleni was another collaboration with the British-born director Peter York.* York has had a steady, but unremarkable career. Its highlight for movie buffs is that he directed Steve McQueen in Bullitt in 1968, a film chiefly remembered for its stomach-churningly intense car chase through downtown San Francisco, with McQueen piloting a Ford Mustang GT (in fact, a stunt man doubled most of the dangerous stuff – Bud Ekins, the same guy who jumped the fence on a motorbike for McQueen in The Great Escape). While York clearly had a soft spot for classic sports cars (one of the smart college kids in Breaking Away drives a Mercedes convertible), Dave's Campag-equipped red Masi Gran Criterium is the hero of the 1979 film.

The non-dialogue scene that is immortal for cyclists is Dave's training ride where he catches the slipstream of a big semi-trailer (fortuitously – or rather, in 70s product-placement-style – badged Cinzano). Beautifully shot, the truck barrels through the flat cornfields of Indiana, with Dave spinning his 13 sprocket like a man possessed, the driver signalling first 50mph, with five fingers, and then, with some dramatic licence, 60mph with five plus one. Finally, the semi gets pulled over for a speeding violation, and Dave coasts into Bloomington's city limits. He checks his watch and smiles to himself – because he knows, and you know, that he'll never do that training run as fast again.

Dennis Christopher, whose boyish charm and beauty hold the centre of the film (against Quaid's angry young man), went

* *No. No. No ... Peter Yates directed Bullitt and other great films.*

148

on to a brisk but undistinguished career, predominantly as a TV actor. Of a film that received five Oscar nominations, only Quaid can be said to have really made it – an ironic outcome, given Breaking Away's preoccupation with who gets to choose their future in the land of the free.

What of Tesich, then, the film's real author?

He was born Stoyan Tesich in the former Yugoslavia, and only moved to the US at the age of 14, following his father, something of a maverick who had rebelled against Tito's regime after military service and managed to escape to Chicago, where he became a machinist. Tesich senior may have bequeathed his son some of his anti-Communist animus, but, in Ray and Dave Stoller, one might also guess at autobiographical echoes, in comedic form, of a stormy father-son relationship. Tesich senior died in 1962, which would have been the year Steve (as he had renamed himself in time-honoured American immigrant fashion) became a freshman at Indiana University. Again, Ray Stoller's heart trouble in the movie may be the pale shadow of a darker story in Steve's real life.

In real life, too, Tesich was one of the college kids, not a "cutter" – although, after only five years in America and having arrived without a word of English, he must still have felt enough of an outsider to be able to recreate, later, the townies' sense of alienation from the gilded existence of the frat boys and sorority girls.

Tesich was a keen athlete, discovered cycling, and in 1962 rode for the Phi Kappa Psi team in the Little 500. The Little 500 continues to this day, having celebrated its 50th anniversary in 2000. A team relay event, just as in the film, it is run around a cinder track, over 200 laps, on single-speed bikes. It's rough and chaotic, a kind of cross between a Madison-style track race and cycle speedway. Just as with Mike's Cutters team, Steve Tesich found himself on the winning squad in 1962. His team-mate, David Blase, set a record by riding 139 of the 200 laps, crossing the line as victor.

Blase told the story, in an interview on National Public Radio's All Things Considered, in 2000, of how the first time he met Tesich was on a training ride in the hills around Bloomington when he rode up to Steve while "singing an aria from Rigoletto". If Steve put some of himself into the character of Dave Stoller, Dave Blase evidently provided the explicit model: "Nothing moved me more than the Neapolitan songs and the arias from operas," he explained – nothing, that is, apart the Italian bikes and kit that were so in vogue after the Rome Olympics of 1960. A nice touch is that Tesich's debt to Blase was subtly acknowl-edged as the credits reveal that the sports announcer for the movie version of the Little 500 is played by a certain David K Blase – a job of commentating he's actually done many times since. And he still rides the 60 miles down from Indianapolis, where he works as a biology teacher, to the race in Bloomington every year: "It's a re-enactment of my youth."

After graduating, Tesich moved to New York to study at Columbia; there, he started to write plays. He had a couple put on at the American Place Theater in the early 70s, but his attempt to break into Broadway, Division Street, flopped. He did succeed in getting some TV drama scripts produced, and started to look towards screenwriting. The script for Breaking Away, though, was his big break, and Oscar success opened doors. He never produced another original screenplay to rival it, but enjoyed a modest hit in 1982 with his adaptation of the John Irving novel, The World According to Garp – incidentally, one of the first serious roles for Robin Williams, best-known up to that point for being the wacky, likeable alien in Mork and Mindy. But Eleni was panned by the critics, and Tesich's Hollywood career dried up abruptly. Disillusioned with writing for the movies, he moved back to New York and continued writing novels and plays, which were performed off-Broadway.

Tesich's career seems the very pattern of the unsuccessful writer's life: a brief moment of untrammelled success, but essentially a narrative of early promise unfulfilled, followed by long, embittering decline. Perhaps, that is too crude a reading, but Tesich's last novel, Karoo, published shortly after his death (from a heart attack) in 1996, at the age of 53, is suggestive. Saul Karoo is an alcoholic script doctor, a truly fallen soul who is given the job of turning a late auteur's masterpiece into Hollywood schlock. Coarsened as he is, even Karoo finds this work distasteful – but he is nothing if not a hack, feeding the dream machine. The novel's final irony is that Karoo, whose attempts to "script doctor" his personal life have disastrously imploded, is rehired to write the autobiographical screenplay of his shame. It is as sour and sardonic a portrait of the enslavement of creative talent in LA's image factory as you could hope to find.

As a parallel commentary on disenchantment, the other body of work Steve Tesich left behind was the non-fiction he could not get published: several essays, including an open letter to the New York Times, in which he argues, with a cold but cogent fury, that the first casualty of the war in Yugoslavia was truth. One suspects the fact that he was Serbian by birth meant that Tesich was regarded as untouchably partisan, and he was writing at a time when most prominent intellectuals – from New York's Susan Sontag to Paris's Bernard-Henri Lévy – had established that the Bosnian Muslims were the "new Jews" of Europe, facing Holocaust at the hands of a totalitarian regime

(Serbia) by its backing of genocidal guerrilla army (the Bosnian Serbs). A humanitarian and liberal, Tesich was no friend of the Milosevic regime, and certainly no apologist for atrocities such as Srebrenica. But he felt bitterly betrayed by his adopted country, its government and media, for buying into what he saw as a grotesquely simplified dramatisation of the civil war that cast the Serbs as villainous tyrants, the Croatians as innocents who merely yearned for the freedom of self-determination, and the Bosnian Muslims as a defenceless minority oppressed by fascist persecution.

Perhaps, as Pauline Kael wrote almost inadvertently in her trashing of his scriptwriting efforts in Eleni, "This is a case of you can take the boy out of the Yugoslavian village but you can't take the Yugoslavian village out of the boy." But it is impossible to read these powerful polemics without feeling some sympathy for Tesich's position: it was not that he wanted America to take sides – his own "side" was not, in any straightforward sense, Serbian – but that he did expect it to uphold the cause of truth. There is, of course, a looming irony that this protest about the sacrifice of veracity in a news media that had become, for him, a provisional wing of the entertainment industry came from a writer who, at times, had marred his own work with crassly idealistic patriotics and regaled his public with crude stereotypes of America's enemies. That, surely, could not have been lost on him. To the extent that Karoo contains an element of self-portrait, it may contain his rueful recognition of the part he himself has played in the monstrous truth-eating machine.

It seems a long way from Breaking Away to Tesich's untimely death, amid anger and disappointment. But when you look closely, the dark apprehensions were already there: Dave Stoller's loss of faith in all things Italian foretold Steve Tesich's rage at what America seemed to him to have become – the slightly paranoid sense that there would always be some superior bastard ready to stick his pump in your wheel and dump you bleeding in the gravel. The sad thing is that Tesich lost that original "cocky humor" – and with it, the idea that there are some things in life you can fix. Like Dave Stoller, you just need a spoke key to make it true.

EIGHT

FURTHER AFIELD: RURAL RIDES AND OTHER ESCAPES

*The bridge from being a Monday-to-Friday pedal-pusher to a week-
end and holiday recreational cyclist and tourist is a natural one.
Once you've made that first commitment, not to turn your cycling
to the purposes of pleasure and fitness seems almost a wilful self-
deprivation. If you run the gauntlet of city streets, why wouldn't
you want to enjoy the rewards of country lanes?*

*And getting out of the Smoke has been one of the motives and
privileges of cycling ever since the bicycle became part of the story
of the industrial revolution. Once a bike could be bought for about
the same price as a suit, it became synonymous with escape and
temporary respite from the rigours of wage slavery in factory and
office – a way of leaving behind "those dark Satanic mills" to visit
"England's green and pleasant land", as William Blake's lyric has
it. Before the motor car, which, arguably, is inimical to those
"pleasant pastures" and "mountains green", only the railways had
accomplished anything like the revolution in democratic access to
the countryside that the bicycle brought in.*

*For me, and for many like me, the weekly excursion beyond the
burbs by bike is a vital means of replenishing both physical and*

mental health. I'm a cheerful city-dweller, not a back-to-nature nut, but my life would be immeasurably impoverished if I did not have this contact with a world beyond the concrete, brick and glass of our built environment. This is one of the bicycle's greatest gifts – and it's free for all.

Thursday April 5, 2007

"It is by riding a bicycle that you learn the contours of a country best, since you have to sweat up the hills and coast down them. Thus you remember them as they actually are, while in a motor car only a high hill impresses you, and you have no such accurate remembrance of country you have driven through as you gain by riding a bicycle."

I've often thought this, and may have said as much. So it's almost annoying to find the idea put into words already. And by Ernest Hemingway, too – not even a noted cyclist. And while we're at it, Ernesto, that first sentence has a nice swing, but the second is a bit clumsy, flabby even; not one of your best, old man.

Hemingway is entirely right, though. There is no finer way of seeing the countryside than by bike. Hiking is fine for rambling types, although I submit that going downhill is a lot more comfortable on a bicycle than on foot (not to mention, quicker). But only the most intrepid and athletic of walkers covers the kind of distance that allows you not only to admire views but to see real changes in landscape.

A typical weekend ride for me takes me out over the chalk escarpment of the North Downs, then up and over the "Greensand Ridge" of the High Weald, and beyond to the rolling, clay-based Kentish Weald. Each geological zone has its characteristic flora, which even a botany-illiterate like me can hardly fail to notice and appreciate. You know, for instance, that you have arrived in a subtly different ecology when you ride up Brasted Chart to Toy's Hill and past the Scots pines and rhododendrons that seem to flourish on the more acidic, sandy soil.

And perhaps that finer register suggests something that Hemingway's aperçu does not pick up. It is not only that the bicycle rider gains a greater feel for landscape than the motorist, but he or she can also retain something of the walker's close observation. On a bike, you are not sealed in an air-conditioned, sound-systematised box; you are moving more slowly, seeing more, hearing and smelling your ambient surroundings. You have not lost that degree of intimacy with the field and hedgerow.

Before I get too rhapsodic, it must be admitted that a ride in the countryside is not necessarily a rural idyll. The creeping suburbanisation of many "greenfield" sites increasingly means that too many country lanes have become rat runs. The only way to enjoy your ride in pristine conditions – and to see much fauna as well as flora – is to set off very early, before people stir themselves for their trips to the DIY store, the golf course, or the car-boot sale.

And speaking of wildlife, what hits your nostrils is less likely to be the scent of a fox than the putrifying cadaver of a badger. Roadkill accounts for all too many of the sightings of birds and mammals. On the other hand, we could dine handsomely most Sundays if I remembered to carry a rucksack for all the pheasants you see, freshly culled by the roadside before any fee-paying businessman has had a chance to fire off a volley (incidentally, distributing about 75,000 metric tonnes of lead around the country every year).

"Et in Arcadia ego" goes the saying: death may stalk here, it's true, but for a city-dweller, these rural rides are also a lifeline, a breath of fresh air, an organic connection. We have a long weekend and a good forecast – what better excuse do you need to go learn some contours?

Wednesday July 19, 2006

Seeing George Bush going for a spin on his mountain bike while attending the G8 summit in St Petersburg almost made my heart warm to him. That's a real lump-of-concrete roadblock of an "almost", but a bit of me does identify with him – the bit that can't bear to go anywhere without a bike, or go for more than a day without a ride.

I don't suppose Bush explored much of St Petersburg itself, which is a shame, because there is no better way to discover an unfamiliar city than by bike: imagine the pleasure of bowling down Nevsky Prospect with a following breeze. No doubt the president preferred to find an off-road trail, as he did when he visited Beijing last year. Which makes the mind boggle at the conversations that must take place between the president's secret service detail and the local police force:

"The president will require a fully secured 10-mile loop including a couple of gnarly downhills and plenty of sweet singletrack."

"Izvineetye?"

Travelling with a bike must be easy if you have your own plane. Presumably Air Force One has enough room for Bush to wheel his bike on without having to break it down and bag it. He probably even has someone to do the wheeling-on bit. But for any of us, in fact, flying with a bike is counter-intuitively easy. Most airlines do not charge, although some levy up to £25. British Airways recently caused consternation among cyclists by announcing new baggage regulations that appeared to exclude bike-sized items. But BA's press office confirms that bikes can still be checked in just as before, at no extra charge, and – better than before – without it even counting towards the overall personal allowance of 23kg.

It is a good idea to buy a padded bag: baggage handlers may be lovely people, but they don't as a rule seem to have that tender feeling for the fragile bits of bicycles and their paintwork that their owners do. Beyond that, the only mechanical task to master is taking off the wheels. And contrary to what some airline staff – and even the formerly misinformed Bike Doctor (never believe him!) – may have told you, you do not even need to let the air out of the tyres, as cargo holds, too, are pressurised.

Absurdly, then, it can be easier to fly with a bike than it is to take one on a train. Not that I particularly want to encourage flying; just the cycling bit. Our family holiday this year is going to involve neither flying nor driving, but going as foot passengers on a ferry to Brittany with our bikes. Guess who gets to tow the luggage on a trailer?

Fair enough, I suppose, as it was my idea. But the baggage allowance may be a bit less than 23kg.

Wednesday November 16, 2005

A few days ago I found myself in Tring with time to kill (it's a long story). A small town in Hertfordshire, about 35 minutes out of London by rail, Tring nestles in a fold at the northern end of the Chiltern hills. Tring: great to say, but not much to do. But I was prepared: I had my bicycle, and the forecast was for a crisp, clear autumnal day of rare perfection.

Cyclists fall into two types: those who hate hills, and those who love them. No prizes for guessing which camp I'm in. Checking the map, I didn't need to see contour lines to work out where they were. To the east lay a series of Tring-like towns – Chesham, Amersham, High Wycombe; to the west, Wendover, Princes Risborough, Chinnor. Ancient names. This is an old part of England, settled and farmed for two millennia and more. Today it is commuter belt, but between these market towns turned dormitory suburbs runs a north-south axis of sparsely populated country, crisscrossed mainly by unmarked minor roads – old droveways no doubt.

The Chilterns are not hugely dramatic hills. From the east, the escarpment is so gentle you hardly realise you are climbing, until suddenly you find yourself on Bledlow Ridge, a high bluff with views all the way to Oxford. You'll know it if you've ever driven in to London on the M40, but believe me, that's hardly the best way to see it. The beauty of the Chilterns is that, unlike many of Britain's upland landscapes, they are well wooded. The low autumnal sun striking the yellows, reds and browns of the still turning leaves bathes the woodlands in shades of gold.

When you watch a kestrel wheeling above you in the chill breeze as you pedal up one of these quiet lanes, you can have the illusion that all this has been put here just for you. In reality, refugees from the Smoke have been coming here to ease their souls with its beauty and solitude for a century or more. There's something nourishing in that, too, to know you're sharing it, riding in their tracks.

Wednesday January 4, 2006

If you're lucky enough to live with the countryside on your doorstep, bully for you. For us city-dwellers, however, the pastures pleasant of rural life can be the best part of an hour away by bike. Which is why green spaces are such a godsend.

In this case, I have in mind Richmond Park. At 955 hectares, Richmond Park is definitely a lot of green space. In fact, it is Europe's largest urban walled park – walls first built in 1637 by Charles I, who brought his court to Richmond to escape an outbreak of the plague in London. Nowadays, the plague is slightly less of a factor, but the park is a popular oasis for urbanites of all stripes, and cyclists in particular.

I was there last week, during the cold snap, and it was pleasant riding. The only real obstacle was the line of cars slowing down for the south-west London safari experience – deer-stalking in 4x4s – but at least it meant they were obeying the 20mph limit for once. To be fair, the deer are picturesque. They come in two types: fallow and red. The fallow deer are not much bigger than a large dog, but even in this smaller species, the stags look pretty magnificent; the antlers on the shaggier red deer are decidedly scary.

But the human wildlife is distractingly exotic too. There are the dog-owners and walkers. Then the joggers and runners, whippet-like in their nervy leanness. And the portly, middle-aged men on mountain bikes – in shorts and T-shirts despite the near-freezing temperature. How do they do that?

The majority of cyclists stick to the road circuit, a lap of about seven miles. On the long drag up from Richmond Gate, I overhauled another cyclist; we ended up riding together for a time. I admired his bike, which was obviously brand-new. "It's titanium," he replied. But I knew that already.

Because this is how evolved we human males are: we don't need to establish status by displaying huge horny growths on our heads like those dumb old deer. That's what we have bikes for.

Saturday January 6, 2007

There is something a bit special about the London to Brighton, though it's far from the most picturesque bike excursion in Britain. The roads are not the quietest. It's not even the most challenging ride you can find. Still, it has something besides a good look at the incredibly plush (thanks to Tom, John and Hollywood friends) Scientology centre near East Grinstead, just off the A22.

For the thousands who do the charity ride every summer to raise money for the British Heart Foundation, covering the distance is the big achievement. I haven't actually clocked it on a bike computer, but it is usually quoted at 58 miles. I tend to think of it as slightly less, but hey, maybe if you make it right down to the seafront and then ride up and down the promenade a bit, it really is.

The other element of the satisfaction is that, just two or three miles outside Brighton city limits, you have to negotiate the obstacle of the South Downs in the shape of the famous – or, possibly, infamous – Ditchling Beacon. This is a mile-long climb that traverses the northern escarpment, rising in a series of winding steps of 10%-14% gradient. As ascents go it's not exactly alpine, but after 50-something miles, it's testing enough for most cyclists.

The views back over your left shoulder as you near the top are wonderful, but the narrow road is, apparently, so jammed on the day of the charity ride that most people have to concentrate hard on weaving a way through the hordes of others who, defeated by the slopes, are pushing their bikes up the hill. This, by the way, is why I always take a day off work, mid-week, to do this ride at another time. That, and because I'm too cheap to pay the registration fee for the organised one.

Ditchling Beacon is a landmark year-round. For many months of the year, there is an ice-cream van in the car park at the top. One good thing about the habitual gale blowing on top is that the windchill factor will stop your Cornetto melting too quickly on all but the warmest day. But take note also of the word "Pantani" still just visible on the road near the top – a tribute to the great Italian climber, painted by fans when the Tour de France last came to Britain in 1994. (The reminder is all the more poignant now, as Marco Pantani died in 2004, amid disgrace and depression, of a cocaine overdose in a hotel in Rimini.)

But an ice cream costs money, so we eschew that. To do this ride, though, you have to eat and drink. The body simply doesn't do these miles without fuel, so fill a bottle or two to carry on your bike, and make a sandwich and take some fresh or dried fruit. You already had this stuff in your fridge, so that's as good as free. Actually, there's a special pleasure in being self-sufficient for a ride like this; even more so if you master the art of eating and drinking on the move (tip: you need one of those cycle jerseys with pockets on the back).

So, by now, you've probably spotted what you think is the logical flaw in this great "free" trip. You ride to Brighton, but then you have to get back to London. By train, by car, whatever ... it costs money.

Uh-uh. You ride home. That's right: it's downhill to Ditchling and then it's just rolling countryside, generally with the wind behind. Imagine how you'll impress your friends with a 100-plus-mile ride.

You think I'm a macho bike nut? Let me tell you, then, that a 16-year-old girl named Tessie Reynonds cycled to London and back in 1893. It took her eight-and-a-half hours (a decent time today). And the fact that she was wearing "rational" dress caused more of a stir than the feat itself. So no excuses: don those knickerbockers and get on your bike!

Thursday November 9, 2006

It was a weird sensation suddenly to have no sensation in my toes once again. The previous week, I had been out riding in shorts and a short-sleeved jersey in the surreally balmy conditions of late October that now pass for post-climate-change autumn (who needs Indian summers any more?). Just one week on, the hedgerows were frosted white, the fields carpeted in a low, freezing mist, and I was grateful the roads were bone-dry so as not to have to worry about the possibility of icy patches. I had almost forgotten what cycling in winter felt like.

I love those sharply cold, but brilliantly bright days. They come rarely enough in this country, where the default weather between October and March is a crepuscular gloom of cloud and penetrating damp chill. But for the cyclist the passage of seasons adds an entire, bike-specific dimension to the biennial wardrobe changeover. What gloves to wear, for instance? Can you get away with mitts for a while longer or do you need the full-finger ones? Is it so cold you need to wear those earwarmers under your helmet or will your head feel like a steamed pudding after 10 minutes if you do?

Ah, dilemmas, dilemmas. But there are many things I like about riding in winter. It is possible, for instance, to ride briskly yet arrive at your destination pleasantly glowing, rather than slick with perspiration, as happens in the summer. Being a typical bike-stuff fetishist, I love my winter jacket with its capacious rear pockets and snug fit. I appreciate how well-designed my gloves are, with the reflective strips on the back of the hands so my signals can be seen and their tailored shape so that they naturally take the curve of your fingers on the bars. I enjoy the feeling of cold air rushing past my face while my head is wrapped warmly in a fleece watch cap. And don't even get me started on the joy of my merino-lined waterproof socks.

The downside is obvious. Now and again, you get wet. And you have to carry all this extra clobber, because you can't afford to be without a rainproof, lights, gloves, hat, on top of the pump, lock and whatnot you have to tote year-round. You also need to take the defensive-riding imperative to a whole new level when you ride in the dark. Your bike can be lit up like a Christmas tree and you yourself luminously dressed to the point of inducing nausea in passers-by, but you can't take for granted that you will be seen by motorists. And when it's dark and wet, it's safest to assume that you might as well be wrapped in Harry Potter's invisibility cloak.

But stick with it, and you will be rewarded. It's best not to shout about it, but the body heat you generate while cycling in winter is as nothing compared with the warmth of inner satisfaction you experience. While everyone else is skipping the gym and over-indulging, you keep your regular exercise habit and top up your Vitamin D by cycling. Believe me, there is nothing like being quietly smug to keep you snug.

NINE

THE WAY OF THE WHEEL: BACKPOCKET PHILOSOPHY

If there is a pitfall for the thinking cyclist, it is the risk of indulging in whimsy. Perhaps it comes from the habit of exploring byways, as the natural mental analogue of wanting to get off the beaten track and follow the road less travelled. But I've seen it happen a little too often in writing about cycling — authors presuming on their readers' willingness to join them in some idio-syncratic passage of thought about life, the universe and the bicycle.

So that is my health warning on this chapter of pieces where I may have overreached myself by trying to be "deep" about what is, finally, just a bloody bicycle.

But having made that disclaimer, let me immediately excuse myself by arguing that you don't have to be a paid-up transcen-dentalist to want to invest larger significance in the day-to-day activities that fill our lives; it is only human. For all our evolu-tionary sophistication, modernity and technology, we remain, in many respects, primitive animists in our feelings about the objects and possessions that are precious to us. If the bicycle is a part of your life, some portion of your identity and personality is bound up with the experience of cycling. It is impossible not to carry around with you a bundle of ideas, concepts and emotions about your bike – many elements of which you may share and have in common with the rest of us who cycle. Most of us have this experience from childhood through adulthood, and it can mean a great deal to us as individuals.

So, if cycling is significant to you, then what, in fact, does it signify? Like most philosophical questions, it may be more important to ask it than to suppose that there are any final or complete answers. Although I think I have just provided quite a good justification for a deal of whimsy.

Wednesday October 18, 2006

As a rule, I don't do magical thinking. I'm not superstitious. I don't recognise supernatural phenomena. I don't even read horoscopes. My attitude is that there's enough unreason in the world without me adding to it.

But the one part of my life where my rationalist forcefield goes on the blink is cycling. When it comes to the bike, my belief system goes haywire. It's not just that I have "lucky shoes" when I race (and lucky socks, mitts and shorts, too) – it's also that whenever anything goes wrong, it is loaded with meaning for me.

Take punctures. You can go for months without one, then suddenly you get three within a week, or on one day, even. Explain that without resort to a notion of providence.

No problem, says the rationalist: punctures happen for two reasons: first, wet weather washes more flints and shards on to the road, and then they work their way in to damp tyres more easily; second, worn tyres are more susceptible and yours probably need replacing.

Nice try ... so why can I not escape the conviction that, at the very least, a puncture is intended as a lesson that you can never take anything for granted and that, if you do, you're bound to take a fall? In fact, as I pump up a tyre by the side of the road, I am searching my conscience for some specific misdeed for which this is a punishment. This usually takes less time to resolve than the repair itself. Because it's so obvious: when you get a flat, it's your karma.

And that's just punctures. If your chain snaps, or you break a spoke, or worse ... well, it's clearly time for some serious soul-searching. On Sunday, my seatpost snapped. The rationalist – O siren voice! – would say that this was hardly surprising, as I was hacking around a cyclo-cross course, a pastime that takes a heavy toll on rider and machine alike. But as I trudged home-ward, head bowed in chagrin, with my crippled, saddleless bike, I knew better: this was atonement. I'm not sure what for, but I'll think of something.

Sure, you'll say, we all ride about with our invisible panniers of guilt. These are the tricks the mind plays, searching for mean-ing – an archetypal narrative – among essentially random events. Or rather, events that may have a logical explanation, but no emotional significance. All very plausible. But the more I cycle, the more I am struck by how it seems an ever more metaphor-ical, even metaphysical, exercise. All life's ups and downs seem mirrored by what happens to you on your bike. Not for noth-ing is samsara, the cycle of birth, life and death, known in Buddhism as "the wheel of suffering".

That said, I'm sure you can get to nirvana by bike, too. In fact, there may be no other way.

Wednesday December 21, 2005

Scarcely a day goes by when I don't use my bike. Mindful of carbon footprints, I consciously avoid using the car whenever possible. Even the weekly trip to the supermarket is now more often done with the help of a bike trailer.

But this is not, smugly, to advertise my green credentials, because – in reality – it's more a matter of preference than eco virtue. I long since pedalled into a realm where cycling ceased to be merely a convenient method of getting from A to B. It's way beyond that. Scarcely a day goes by when I don't use my bike because, to be honest, I just hate it when I don't.

It's not about the exercise: I barely break a sweat for my 20-minute commute. But it gives me something I need. A deep physical pleasure, certainly. I love the rhythm of the pedalling cadence; I find it soothing and calming. I don't ride particularly fast, but there is still the sensation of speed, the satisfaction of moving under one's own steam.

A great sense of mental wellbeing, too. Somehow, I always seem to arrive at my destination with my head centred, my priorities clearer. And having travelled without being cut off from the environment. Sure, there is a downside: instead of being cocooned in a car's comfy, air-conditioned, music-filled compartment, you are fully exposed to the elements, and to the noise and grime of the city.

But the upside is that you see so much and experience it far more vividly. The other day, I cycled along a road not normally on my route, but one I have driven down 100 times. I looked up at a nondescript Victorian house I'd hardly noticed before and saw, on the second floor, two alcoves set in the wall in which sat a plaster-of-paris owl and pussycat. Who knows what their story is, but they made me laugh out loud.

A day without cycling feels incomplete, a day wasted. You could say I'm a bicycle cultist, a cycling obsessive, a bike freak. But do you know what you're missing?

Wednesday August 16, 2006

"The difference between us," says my wife, Anna, "is that if I were to go cycling, it would have to be flat, and if there were any hills, I'd get off and walk. Whereas, if you go cycling, you go looking for hills." This is true. I would consider it scarcely worth getting togged out to go for a bike ride if there weren't some hills to be climbed. During my mid-life lay-off from cycling (otherwise known as having a young family), any trip or holiday that took us near mountainous country would have me looking up wistfully at the distant blue hills and dreaming what it would be like to ride among them.

The lure of the hills is partly about the need for a physical challenge, partly also about the panoramic views they reward that effort with. But it is also a soul thing. About lifting your spirit up from the common, quotidian life of the plain and searching for something transcendant. Mountains, as the Romantics knew, are sublime.

OK, so Caspar David Friedrich would have been thinking of something a bit more vertiginous than the North Downs or the Chilterns, but you take what you can get and, for the rest, there is the imagination. I can think of at least two country lanes among the Surrey hills known to cyclists as the "Little Alps". A little aspirational, perhaps, but we all need a dream to nurture.

Not all cyclists fantasise about hills, I accept. And I mean no snobbery by it: I don't consider people who like hills "proper cyclists" and others not. If it were a choice between living in a pan-flat country where practically everyone went by bike and a gorgeously hilly one where most people drove, I'd choose Holland every time. I guess I'd put up with headwinds instead of hills. And book holidays in the Dolomites.

But there is another side to this hill-seeking. "Isn't life uphill enough already?" asks Anna. Meaning, why make things harder for yourself? I've thought about this, and I think I like riding uphill because, if you can conquer that climb, then the uphill business of getting through life seems easier. My cycling is a hobby and a sport, and so, like all such pastimes, a displacement activity – yes, a way of avoiding more difficult things. But it also has a metaphorical quality. The title of a (sadly not very good) documentary film about the 2004 Tour de France currently on release is Overcoming. A bit pompously Nietzschean, but you get the idea.

There is an obvious fallacy in the idea that an ability to ride a bike up a long, hard hill in any way equips you for the infinitely more complex and challenging stuff of life. But if it lifts the spirit to climb that mountain, perhaps it is a useful illusion.

Thursday April 12, 2007

Even when he's not insulting whole cities (or "towns", as he might say), one wouldn't necessarily want to endorse everything Boris Johnson says, militant cyclist though he is. He has practically cornered the market in the politically incorrect soundbite. At a recent meeting in Islington, for example, he called for "Sharia law for bicycle thieves". It's hard to imagine David Cameron ever appointing Boris home secretary with that quote waiting to haunt him.

Yet we do have Boris to thank for successfully opposing an

amendment to legislation that would have enabled police to prosecute cyclists for using a handheld mobile phone while riding, as they can motorists for doing so while driving. Not that I'm saying that using a mobile while cycling is a smart idea – but it's good to know you can't be done for it, if you do.

This perhaps falls into the category of what could be thought of as cycling's illicit pleasures: things you can do on a bike that you probably shouldn't, but which you do because they're too much fun. I'm afraid I'm a serial sinner in this regard, and I'd like several offences to be taken into account.

Item one: riding "no hands". My journey to work begins on a long, straight, broad road, and I'm always in a rush, so I hop on to my bike and then – when I'm already under way – need to fiddle around finding my dark glasses or putting on gloves or getting my iPod sorted (and that's a whole other sin, but let's not get started on that one). So I ride the first quarter-mile hands-free. It's probably not very sensible. Conceivably, even, I could get pulled over for riding without due care and attention. But I do it all the same. Because I can, and because I get a kick out of it.

Item two: "trackstands". My favourite little game with myself on my commute is not to put a foot down the whole way. So I'm the guy you see at the lights balancing stationary, which is probably very irritating because it looks as though I'm just showing off. But I'd actually argue that by working on your balance, it improves your bike-handling generally. Oh, and it's absolutely addictive. Master this skill and a whole universe of circus tricks opens in front of you: from winning slow riding races (really, they exist), to cycling backwards in circles (I've seen it done).

Item three: "bunny-hopping". A handy way of riding up kerbs and other obstacles without mashing your rims. Not very sensible on the face of it, but actually a useful ability if it means you can "jump" a pothole in an emergency. And again, idiot fun.

All very childish, I know – it's not responsible, adult behaviour. But that's the point: one of the joys of cycling is the reconnection with that childhood spirit of freedom from constraint. Can that be wrong?

Thursday January 4, 2007

A few days before Christmas, I did someone a good turn, in that slightly self-conscious, Frank Capra-esque way that you do these things. On my way home from work, over Blackfriars bridge, in London, a young woman was working at a wheel on the pavement next to her up-ended bicycle. It was cold – and even in these post-climate change winters, the middles of bridges over the Thames are good places to feel cold – and I was late getting back already. But as I went past, I asked if she was all right.

She probably said she was fine, thanks, but the wind caught her answer. It took me a few more pedal revolutions (my brain being permanently stuck in a big gear) to work out that if I hadn't heard her response, then there was a possibility – albeit unlikely, given prevailing local English customs of denial – that it might have been one of desolation and distress. In which case, to ride on would be the ultimate in callous disregard. In which case, I really needed to stop and see if she needed help.

Turned out she did. She was evidently a competent cyclist, as she was wearing proper cycling gear. She had already managed to repair the puncture, she said, but was just stuck trying to get the tyre fitted back on to the rim, which is not easy to do with small hands and frozen fingers. So I did that bit and, not wishing to be patronising, left her to pump it up and put the wheel back in.

So much for good Samaritanism, and this, in any case, is not the point of the anecdote. Rather the opposite. How often have I ridden past other commuters forlornly pushing their bikes, prompting me to make a visual note that, yes, they do have a flat tyre or a hopelessly enmeshed chain? I can think of one other instance, last year, when I stopped to aid a stranger. I gave a guy with a flat my spare inner tube, refusing even to take payment for it (this I regretted five minutes later, when I went into a bike shop to replace it).

What made me stop in these two cases, when so often I've passed by, no doubt quickening my pace the sooner to escape my own bad odour of mingled smugness and guilt at consciously refusing the charitable act? It's as arbitrary, I realise, as when I choose to give money to homeless people. Sometimes I do, furious at the injustice of a society that obliges people to beg. Other times, I don't, furious at the injustice of a society that obliges people to give to beggars.

So my new year's resolution is to show more moral consistency in stopping and offering other cyclists help. But if your chain's off, forget it. I will help you with your puncture, but I'm not getting my hands covered in grease for anyone. That's consistent enough.

from Rouleur, vol.3, 2006

INTIMATIONS OF MORTALITY: DEATH ON A BIKE
When was your last near-miss?

Mine came this season past in a road race. I had just been pulling hard in a small group that was working to prise itself off the front of the bunch. We'd just reached a fast downhill section, and I took the opportunity to take a drink. Perhaps the fatigue of the preceding minutes' extreme effort cost me a momentary lapse of concentration, for, reaching down, I fumbled for my bottle and had to look. I didn't wobble, but taking my eyes of the road made me alter my line slightly. At 40mph, it was enough – in a fraction of a second – to take me a foot or so closer to the centre line. When I looked up, the next instant, I was almost ready to bounce off the side of a van coming the other way. I flicked the bike back on track, but not before I'd felt the draft from the van's wing mirror on my face; I was that close.

So what? Nothing happened. What should I have done: climbed off my bike and, there on the verge, sworn to take up some safer pastime, like bridge or bowls? Of course not. I accepted the adrenaline hit gratefully, put it out of my mind and got on with the race. I don't think I'd even thought about it again until now.

But there it is. Cycling is a dangerous sport. Even when not conducted as a sport, cycling is not without risk. Who among us who rides a bike has not lain awake at night and sweated through those bad imaginings of what might have happened if, on that fast descent that had earlier made our heart race not with fear but with joy, the front tyre had suddenly blown out just as we carved the apex of that glorious curve?

We cannot pretend to ourselves that such things never happen. We know that to cycle is, in some unwilling, unac-knowledged way, to accept that we might die. Death is a possibility, how remote we cannot tell. None of us are so super-stitious as to believe that death lurks around the next corner, yet all of us are rational enough to know that it might.

I do not believe there is any serious cyclist who has not thought about it seriously. Most of the time when we ride, it is the knowledge we put in our back pocket, out of sight. It is the movement glimpsed out of the corner of the eye, not quite in our field of vision. It is the word whispered just out of earshot. Death stalks us as we cycle: we know it, but we choose not to think about it.

And it is the great unknowable. How can we quantify the risk we run in any meaningful way? The science of accident statistics does not help us. It tells us reassuringly that cyclist fatalities are, in the grand scheme of "per million passenger-kilometres", extremely rare. Each of us, it says, would have to cycle millions of kilometres and for thousands of years in order, finally, for our luck to run out and for us to be packed off to bike nirvana by a clip from an artic.

Yet all of us know someone in cycling who has died, some of us perhaps several. Commonly enough when we race, the event is a memorial to some rider less lucky. Look around the room where people are changing, rubbing in warm-up balm, pinning numbers to their jerseys: how many are contemplating mortality? At that moment, none. But that reckoning comes: you can race as fast as you like, but you cannot for ever outrun the thought that, one day, maybe sooner, maybe later, it will all come to an end.

For a few, a very few, it might end violently on the road. The freak fatalities that have occurred during races – such as the deaths of Fabio Casartelli and Andrei Kivilev – are memorialised as the heroes of foreign wars would be. The traffic incidents that took people we knew – Simon Hook, Zak Carr, and the members of Rhyl CC (Thomas Harland, Maurice Broadbent, Dave Horrocks and Wayne Wilkes) – seem more modest, domestic tragedies. For most of our community, the club cyclists remembered in brief obituaries in the weekly press, it will be an ordinary exit after an ordinary span, probably attended by the usual ailments and infirmity.

But what kind of end could a cyclist want? As I ride along a country lane, I sometimes think of Beryl Burton, arguably the greatest female cyclist this country has produced. She died, too young at 58, in 1996. The manner of her death, though, was one any *coureur* might envy. She was found at the side of the road, by her bike, having apparently suffered heart failure while out on a training run.

There is nothing romantic about death; it is always a loss, a removal, a taking-away – and all too often, untimely. But as what we do when we ride is assert our health, our strength and our pleasure, we tend to accept the risks we run. To feel more alive, even in the face of threat or danger, is to affirm life itself.

Dying exactly as she had lived, and true to type, Burton came closer than most of us will ever manage to outpacing death itself. It still came for her. But she made it chase hard.

TEN

HEALTH AND WHEEL BEING

"Get a bicycle. You will not regret it, if you live," wrote Mark Twain. To be fair, anyone attempting to master an old high-wheeler, as he was, was probably entitled to be a tad sardonic about it. It was no accident, so to speak, that when, in 1885, John Starley adapted the chain-drive mechanism for the rear wheel and made a bike with two equal-sized wheels and the rider perched on the frame in between, his design was marketed as the "safety bicycle". It was an inherently more stable ride, and one much easier to master.

Since then, cyclists have enjoyed more than 120 years of health-giving, fitness-boosting exercise – barring, still, the occasional tumble. At the extreme end, professional cyclists are among the most highly trained endurance athletes on the planet: perhaps only rowers and cross-country skiers can rival them for their work ethic and fitness level. At the other end of the spectrum, cycling is an easy, painless and convenient way for people of all ages to get their recommended 30 minutes of exercise a day.

Uncontroversial enough, you would think, yet there are points of friction. Not everyone thinks it's a good idea to put bums on bike seats. Rest assured, though, the benefits of greater cardiovascular fitness far outweigh the problems experienced "down there" by a small minority. Just as the health benefits and greater life

expectancy far outweigh the minute risk of becoming a road traf-
fic accident statistic.

And do helmets help with the latter? An ever vexing subject, on
which I perform (again) a partial U-turn. As I change not only
my mind about it, but also my actual helmet-wearing habit, on an
almost daily basis, the only sensible thing to say is that it should
remain a matter of personal indecision.

Thursday April 26, 2007

Flann O'Brien famously advanced the "Mollycule Theory" in The Third Policeman, according to which "people who spend most of their natural lives riding iron bicycles over the rocky roadsteads of the parish get their personalities mixed up with the personalities of their bicycles as a result of the interchanging of mollycules of each of them." Unfortunately, the truth of the relationship can be a little less romantic.

Down there. It's not the most transcendent of themes, but sooner or later, every cyclist has to deal with it. Not surprisingly, it is a sensitive and touchy subject.

Bum just about covers it, but the vernacular simplifies quite a complex junction. When you sit on a bike saddle, your weight is borne at three pressure points: two are bony, your ischial tuberosities, or "sit bones"; one is soft tissue, the perineum. The difficulty with the latter is that this strip of flesh carries arteries, vessels and nerves that supply the genital area – and which get squeezed when you ride a bike. It is this fact that led a urologist named Dr Irwin Goldstein to make his notorious 1997 claim: "There are only two kinds of male cyclists – those who are impotent and those who will be impotent."

Apart from the fact that even professional cyclists seem able to procreate, one's own anecdotal experience would, it is hoped, suggest that Goldstein was overstating his case. Still, the idea of a link between cycling and erectile dysfunction (ED) took root, so to speak, even though the evidence is at best contradictory. Two Boston-based studies, for instance, found slightly higher rates of ED among cyclists (4%) than among runners (1%) or swimmers (2%). But we would need to know the age of the cyclists concerned, as the rate of impotence in the general population is thought to be about 2% for 40-year-old men and 25% for 65-year-olds, averaging out at perhaps 10% for men of all ages.

Impotence, anyway, is not the whole story; or even part of it, for female cyclists. Such studies as there are suggest that women experience many of the same issues as men: soreness and chafing, "saddle sores" (cysts), and nerve damage and numbness (the "numb nuts" phenomenon, as it is known, among male cyclists). When I interviewed the great Irish cyclist Sean Kelly recently, he told me that he had pain peeing for three days after the Paris-Roubaix race. But that's what you get for riding more than 250km in a day, large chunks of it over murderous cobbles.

Yet it's not all grim down south. These problems are manageable: a bike that fits well, wearing padded shorts and shifting position frequently all help. As does pedalling harder – it means more of your weight is carried by your legs – and avoiding cobbles.

But the real clincher is the mound of medical evidence about the cardiovascular benefits of exercise. One doctor researching exercise and sexual function among men with heart problems compared the effect of cycling to that of Viagra. In general, anyone who exercises is likely to enjoy a better sex life, while obesity, diabetes and heart disease all correlate with ED. Aerobic exercise also helps beat depression, commonly associated with loss of libido.

So, it isn't so bad to be one of those people O'Brien's police sergeant spoke of "who are nearly half people and half bicycles". Perhaps his real point was that cycling, like sex, is as much in the head.

Tuesday January 23, 2007

The bicycle, rightfully, occupies a special place in our affections. In survey after survey, it is voted people's favourite invention of all time. There's no mystique about that: it is a supremely practical device for getting around, ideally suited to modern urban living, where most of our journeys are just a mile or two. It is quick, convenient, cheap, non-polluting and green. But people love their bikes not just because they're useful, but because they bring joy.

Cycling is one of life's great pleasures. For the majority of us, our bikes were our first taste of real freedom and independence, delivering an addictive thrill of speed, which, in the early days of the bicycle, was often likened to flying. And that simple, childlike gratification is something we never lose. In fact, we get to experience it every time we saddle up.

Unlike some forms of physical exertion, what feels good about cycling really is good for us. Cycling is a superb form of exercise, for all ages. Like swimming, cycling involves no impact and is load-bearing, so there is very little risk of injury, compared with running or other sports. It is also highly aerobic: in other words, it gets you out of breath and raises your heart rate, so it is working your cardiovascular system. And that has all sorts of health benefits: it reduces the risk of heart disease and strokes, it lowers blood pressure, it cuts the risk of diabetes, and it burns calories, especially fat, very effectively.

If you only ride 2-3 miles to work and back, five times a week, you will have the fitness of someone 10 years younger. You will also burn the equivalent of 5kg of fat a year. And you'll be meeting the government's recommended target of doing 30 minutes of moderate exercise five times a week – without even having to go to the gym. Just do this and no more, and after a few months you will have put yourself in the fitter half of the population.

You will arrive at work alert, refreshed and feeling ready for whatever the day throws at you. Because, like other forms of aerobic exercise, cycling causes the release of endorphins – your body's natural "feel-good" opiates – which induce a sense of wellbeing, help beat stress and generally improve your mental, as well as your physical, health.

Cycling has even been shown to ameliorate premenstrual symptoms. And good cardiovascular condition correlates with good sexual health. So, not to boast, but it's true: cyclists do it better.

Wednesday August 2, 2006

Amid the gloom that came with the Tour de France winner Floyd Landis's positive drug test was one lighter moment. In one report of the affair, in which Landis showed positive for testosterone after his remarkable solo win in the Alps on stage 17, it emerged that the American was lucky not to have been breathalysed and test positive for alcohol as well.

After his dramatic collapse on the previous day, when he slumped from third to 11th and seemed out of contention, Landis apparently went for a couple of consolatory beers with friends and later knocked back four whiskies. Not exactly what the team doctor would prescribe as a "recovery drink".

Of course, the current predicament of professional cycling makes one more suspicious than ever of being spun a yarn: perhaps the boozing story is meant to quell speculation that Landis might have been given some kind of artificial "pick-me-up" following his disastrous stage 16. But it seems more likely he was just drowning his sorrows.

Tour riders live like monks during the season, denying themselves treats and obsessively managing their weight while burning tens of thousands of calories in the saddle. The temptation to binge, if you think the entire purpose of your season has gone up in smoke, must be almost irresistible.

And for those of us whose livelihood does not depend on keeping our body fat below 5%, the temptation to drink and ride is even stronger. Arguably, one of the unspoken advantages of riding a bike, as opposed to driving a car, is that you can get away with having a couple of beers without losing your licence. This is not to condone drink-riding in the slightest – I know someone who needed extensive dental repairs after crashing into a bollard while cycling drunk – but the working assumption is that, unlike drink-driving a car, the only person the pissed cyclist puts at risk is him or herself.

The problem is, of course, that being able to get away with it doesn't make it a great idea. Well into the 1970s, racers sometimes took a few sips of brandy towards the end of a race, in the belief that the temporary euphoria would aid them, but the truth is that alcohol does not enhance performance. (Even if it was boosted by testosterone, Landis's stage 17 ride now appears all the more miraculous, as he must have had a hangover.) Apart from the burden alcohol places on the metabolism, it also impairs balance and speed of reaction. Most dangerous of all, it disinhibits, encouraging risk-taking behaviour.

I like the "buzz" as much as the next person, but it's a false friend: the last thing we need is to feel invulnerable.

Friday July 1, 2005

This week, the annual meeting of the British Medical Association (BMA) voted to campaign for cycle helmets to be made compulsory.

The last time the BMA voted on this issue, it went against the move to lobby for compulsion. This change of policy immediately drew a chorus of protest from cycling groups, the most prominent being CTC – the UK's national cyclists' organisation – which, with 55,000 members, is the UK's oldest and largest cyclists' organisation.

Their key objection was that making helmet use compulsory would act as a deterrent to many who already do, or who might in future, ride a bicycle. A lack of physical exercise, leading to the present obesity epidemic, is a far greater public health problem, they argued, than the relatively small number of head and facial injuries that might be prevented or mitigated by wearing a helmet.

"The doctors who voted for helmet compulsion may have been well-intentioned, but actually their stance will do far more harm to the health of the nation than any benefit which helmets might have achieved," CTC's director, Kevin Mayne, said.

According to the organisation, even road safety groups not influenced by a special interest in cycling, such as the Royal Society for the Prevention of Accidents and the Parliamentary Advisory Council on Transport Safety, broadly agree with this position.

Some cycling campaigners go further. They not only claim that the evidence for helmets reducing the incidence of head injuries is questionable, but even that cyclists who wear a helmet actually expose themselves to greater risk because they derive an illusory sense of invulnerability from doing so.

Hardliners point out that making cyclists wear helmets is akin to blaming the victim when the goal of making roads safer for cycling, they say, would be better served by making drivers change their behaviour.

I used to find all of the above points persuasive. And while I almost always elected to wear a helmet myself (a habit acquired through racing, in which it is, rightly, compulsory), I took a libertarian view. Wearing a helmet was not something anyone should be compelled to do, and the last thing we needed was another obstacle to discourage people from getting on their bikes.

But I find that I've changed my mind.

Part of this is due to a very concrete discovery of the efficacy of my helmet. Last year, I crashed while racing. I broke my collarbone but, thanks to my helmet, escaped serious facial injury, heavy concussion ... or worse.

Of course, crashing in a race is an occupational hazard – it is an inherently risky activity. But the point is that if you ride a bike – whether commuting through traffic or meandering down country lanes – sooner or later, you too will have a crash. Wet roads, careless opening of car doors, spilt diesel, being a bit drunk (let's be honest, it happens) ... there are endless scenarios for hitting the deck, and one of them will catch up with you down the road.

Modern helmets, by the way, are infinitely better than they used to be: lighter, better designed, and more ventilated. One reason I used to sympathise with the anti-helmet libertarians was because the damn things were hot, heavy and plug-ugly. That reason has gone.

Another, similar mind-changing event was my daughter falling off her bike just a couple of weeks ago. She is a more than averagely competent cyclist for a 10-year-old, but on this occasion was caught out by a badly laid drain cover. Her wheel tramlined and she was thrown off.

She ended up with a grazed elbow and a sore head. Sore, but not broken. The helmet was broken, just as it was designed to be – absorbing the shock and cracking. The fact that she was wearing a helmet made all the difference between being able to get back on her bike and ride home and having to spend the rest of the day in A&E.

Cycle accidents, apparently, account for approximately 20% of all head injuries in children, and an untold amount of emergency dental work.

But I'm not going to get into the statistics game, because both sides in this debate quote stats ad nauseam as though they provide incontrovertible proof of their point of view, and I find them almost always distracting and misleading.

The short answer, which both common sense and experience will tell you, is that helmets work. They actually do what they're supposed to.

The logic here is that children are bound to fall off their bikes. It is completely predictable. Therefore they should wear helmets to protect their heads. For them not to do so would be, for the responsible adult, to place your child unnecessarily in harm's way.

And if this is the case for children, why should adults be allowed to take the risk? I find myself more and more in sympathy with the doctors and dentists who have to patch up the consequences of helmet non-use at considerable cost to the public purse. What social good is accomplished there?

My attitude has gradually migrated from "Well, I wear a helmet but I defend your right not to," via "Why wouldn't anyone in their right mind not wear a helmet?", to "People really should wear helmets." And "should" means it ought to be compulsory.

Of course, there would be problems with enforcement (just look at how many people are still driving one-handed while talking on a handheld mobile phone).

There may even be a fall-off in the number of people cycling. But this would be temporary; people would adjust – wearing a helmet would soon seem as natural as taking your lock and lights with you. Besides, there are many public policy levers that can be pulled to encourage more people to cycle, to compensate for the supposed deterrent effect.

The BMA's move is controversial – many doctors in its own ranks involved in public health policy disagree with the new policy – but the debate is welcome.

The whole cycling environment, and helmets themselves, have changed in recent years. It is time for the cycling lobby to put aside its automatic rejectionism and think again.

Wear a helmet? Hey, Lance does it. As he might say, it's a no-brainer.

Wednesday March 22, 2006

(Deep breath.) Bicycle helmets. This is a subject I have mostly avoided until now. But prevarication can take you only so far, and now it's bothering me like a squeaky chain. So what's the problem, you ask – surely wearing a helmet equals safer cycling? Sadly, nothing is so straightforward.

As we pedalled out into the Surrey Hills early on Sunday morning, my clubmate Ben told me about a spectacular crash he'd had in a race last year. (If you race, helmets are compulsory.) "My helmet split in half like a walnut," he said, but he walked away from the spill. I've shattered a helmet myself this way. I had to stay in hospital overnight for observation, but I'm in no doubt that my helmet saved me from serious concussion or worse. So I generally keep the habit of wearing a helmet at all times. But that Sunday Ben just had a woolly hat on.

Unless you race, whether or not you wear a helmet is up to you. A few countries have made them compulsory, notably Australia – with mixed results, the main effect being to reduce the number of people who cycle. One study even found that the reduction in head injuries was less than the decline in cycling. This is only to be expected, as all the evidence says that cyclists are safer in numbers. In Holland, for example, a quarter of all journeys are done by bike and the average person pedals more than 10 times further a year than we do; yet the Dutch record only twice as many cycling fatalities.

The most vociferous pro-helmet lobby is the medical establishment. I have some sympathy, as it's the doctors who have to patch us up. But even they can't agree. A 1989 study of cycling casualties in Seattle concluded that helmets reduce the risk of head injury by 85%, but this paper has been much criticised. Another Seattle study reduced the claim to 69%. A review of more than 10 years' data extrapolated a risk reduction of only 45%. While, in 2001, a US government agency reported that, as cycling declined and helmet use increased over the previous decade, head injuries rose by 10%. Go figure.

Confusion rules. One British paper famously argued that helmet-wearing can cause casualties by making cyclists feel invulnerable and take greater risks. But this is contradicted by another study, which found that people who wear helmets are also more likely to stop at lights and use hand signals. The benefit of helmet use being hard to quantify, the government's own Transport Research Laboratory has not even tried. While the anti-helmeteers may protest too much, the reason they do so is because they fear that if the case for helmets were "proved", then the pressure for compulsory wearing would be irresistible. Net result: fewer cyclists riding at greater risk. And that, as Australians have discovered, is no accident.

Wednesday October 12, 2005

Pretty serious news the other day for cyclists. At least, for chaps who are cyclists. According to US research, riding a bike reduces the blood flow to, ahem, vital regions, causing first numbness, then impotence. In the Journal of Sexual Medicine, Dr Steven Schrader wrote that it was no longer a question of "whether or not bicycle-riding on a saddle causes erectile dysfunction". In other words, it's a fact.

Ouch.

I wish I had more to say, but I suspect that any elaboration on this subject would fall into the more-than-you-wanted-to-know category of confessional journalism. I can't even ventriloquise: I don't have a "close friend" who could tell more. Oddly enough, the conversational gambit "I went for a six-hour ride last weekend and, you know, the damnedest thing, but I couldn't get it up that night," does not have great currency among my cycling acquaintance.

Aside from my lack of competence to comment on it, erectile dysfunction is a serious medical problem, not to be made light of. But there is another type of cycling-related male sexual dysfunction on which, sad to say, I can report: total cycling-obsession syndrome.

It, too, is protected by a conspiracy of silence, although I know that the corrosive misery of this affliction is an unspoken sorrow visited on all too many couples. Consider, for example: that "other" wardrobe of figure-hugging fetish wear. The furtive visits to retail outlets and secret purchases, undisclosed but for the telltale credit-card statements. The untimely early-morning departures for bizarre assignations with nameless mates in seemingly respectable suburbs. The compulsive poring-over of subscription-only specialist publications. The stolen hours of solitary fiddling.

It is a truly distressing condition, this utter sublimation of the male libido. It can strike at any time, but men of a certain age seem particularly vulnerable. For them – and for the women in their lives – the bitter truth is that it is no longer a question of whether or not bicycle riding is to blame. It's a fact.

Thursday March 29, 2007

The signs of spring are with us. The clocks have changed, and March's daffodils will soon give way to April's bluebells. The weather has a softer, warmer touch. And cyclists everywhere are coming out of hibernation.

It can be slightly galling for the hardy types who keep pedalling through the winter, but all of a sudden, it's hard to find a slot in the bike racks at work. And then, by 10am on Sunday morning, there is a queue of Lycra-clad types at the National Trust cafe at the top of Box Hill in Surrey. So where were they in January, eh?

Actually, I don't believe in that snobbery about "fair-weather cyclists". People should ride when they feel like it and when it suits. To be willing to keep the habit through rain, wind, sleet and frost takes a certain mentality: dedication, compulsion, what you will.

Now that people are dusting off their frames and venturing further afield, the counters in bike shops are groaning with the array of nutritional stuff for cyclists: energy bars, gel sachets, drinks powders, all in fabulously synthetic flavours such as "forest fruits", which, one suspects, have very little to do with either forests or fruit.

But then the idea of sports nutrition is not to provide a gourmet experience, but to help you go faster, longer, further. Naturally, that's an aspiration we can all buy into – and we do. It's a big market: sports drinks alone are now worth £1bn in western Europe, while in the UK consumption doubled between 1999 and 2003 (and has probably done so again). And that's before you even peel the wrapper off an energy bar, which costs £1 a pop at least.

Not only profit, but necessity has been the mother of sports nutrition. If you're going on a ride of more than an hour, you should definitely have something with you to drink; and once you're into that second hour, you should be nibbling something solid, too. The body's stores of energy are relatively limited and need replenishing from some handy carbohydrate source. Otherwise you soon discover that your body is not unlike the internal combustion engine: run out of fuel and you grind to a halt very quickly. Cyclists call it getting "the hunger knock" or "the bonk". Though not dangerous, going into a hypoglycaemic state is definitely not a nice feeling and best avoided.

Hence the term "bonk food". The good news is that almost anything edible counts. Fruit, either fresh or dried (for convenience), is pretty ideal. In fact, bananas are so ideal (easy to chew, swallow and digest, and containing potassium, which we easily lose in sweat) that you would think they were designed with cyclists in mind. They slip naturally into those back pockets and even come with a disposable biodegradable wrapper, which is more than you can say for the gel sachets, which too many racers chuck away as if they were somehow not litter that will take several centuries to turn to mulch. Fig rolls are another longstanding staple of cyclists, and will keep you going just as well as the reconstituted and extruded blend of ground nuts, cereal, dried fruit, powdered whey and maltodextrin that's glued together in your expensive energy bar.

And not forgetting that venerable cycling tradition: the cafe stop. They do a great slice of homemade flapjack at Box Hill. Though, possibly, anything would taste good by the time you reach the top.

Wednesday May 10, 2006

It may be cycling's most sensitive subject. Its sore point. I'm talking about the contact between you and your bike – and I don't mean your hands. The arrival of spring, May bank holidays, the longer evenings: all bring the opportunity and incentive to do longer rides. But there is a price to be paid for the pleasures of getting outward bound. Not to be indelicate, but you are likely to get a sore bum.

The good news is that it will pass. In my experience, one's perineum rapidly transforms itself into a piece of old boot leather. Just keep riding, and it gets more comfortable, not less.

And the bad news? Well medical experts are queueing up to tell us chaps that cycling is basically DIY castration in slow motion. Ever since 1997, when a certain Boston urologist and now sexual health guru, Dr Irwin Goldstein, drew a link between bicycle saddles and impotence, there has been a host of studies purporting to show that riding a bike compresses a perineal sheath known as Alcock's canal (I'm not making this up), restricting blood flow to the penis and causing pudendal nerve damage. Possible symptoms: penile numbness, erectile dysfunction, impotence, infertility ...

Definitely in the category of bad news, if true. My standard response is that the propagation of the species does not appear to have ended around 1900, when biking really took off. In fact, today, it is a podium cliche that professional cyclists brandish their latest bambino as they collect their prize. No obvious infertility issues there – and think of all the miles in the saddle they do.

The fascinating thing, though, about this panic is that it mirrors a similar hysteria (I use the term advisedly) about the damage the bicycle would do to women. In the 1890s, it was women whose sexual health came under scrutiny. Certain physicians and self-appointed moral guardians were anxious that the effect of sitting on a saddle might ruin women's "organs of matrimonial necessity", as one writer charmingly put it. The bicycle would vandalise the reproductive apparatus of the "weaker sex". Paradoxically, others were nervous that female "scorchers" – speedy riders – might experience inappropriate sexual arousal from friction with the saddle.

What we read here is an unsavoury confection of fantasies and anxieties about the New Woman. Is it possible that – under the guise of fearing for his sexual wellbeing – what is actually feared is the New Man? The apparent solicitude for the fin-de-siecle female cyclist masked hostility and rage: worry about fertility was in reality a desire to castrate. Is the metrosexual man on his bike so disturbing a social figure that what is wished for is his emasculation?

Wednesday June 7, 2006

My legs are still sore from racing at the weekend. As you get older, one of the things you notice is that the recovery takes a little longer. But at 40, I should still have a few years left in me. Saturday's race was won by Malcolm Elliott, who, at 44, showed a clean pair of wheels to a field in which there were plenty of riders whom he is old enough to have fathered.

When I first got into cycling, Elliott was king: a winner of the Milk Race and the Kelloggs Tour, he was one of the few domestic riders to make an impression on the continent, winning the sprinter's jersey in the 1989 Tour of Spain. His comeback illustrates a theory of mine, that there are two kinds of professional cyclist.

On retirement, one sort locks the bikes in the garage and throws away the key. In the old days, they would open a bar or a shop; now, with more money in the bank, they'll buy a farm or go into business. Either way, nothing to do with bikes. And it's hard to blame them: after 15 or 16 years in which a seven-hour training ride or a 200km race in freezing rain was just another day at the office, that might be enough cycling for any of us.

But then there are the types for whom the fitness that comes with racing is compulsive, the competition addictive. They retire as pros, but they can't give it up. That great Irish rider of the 1980s, Sean Kelly, still turns a pedal in anger now and again.

In my part of the world, Sean Yates – at 46 still as whippet-lean as the day he won the yellow jersey in the Tour de France in 1994 – takes time off from his duties as assistant "*directeur sportif*" for Lance Armstrong's old team to show amateurs such as me what racing really means. For my generation, this is like kicking a ball about the park on a Sunday only to discover that you're supposed to be marking John Barnes.

And it's not only the ex-pros who are reluctant to hang up their wheels: there's a whole geriatric racing scene out there. I belong to an organisation called (I kid you not) the League of Veteran Racing Cyclists. Veteran here just means 40 and over, but there are guys still racing in their 60s and beyond – none of them slouches. And what's to stop them? Unlike soccer, cycling doesn't take such a toll on knees, ankles and groins. Looking around a room full of these "vets" is a bit like a game of exquisite corpse: grey heads and bald pates grafted improbably on to lithe, athletic bodies that would not disgrace a 20-year-old.

It can be a bit dispiriting to keep getting stuffed in races, year after year, by the same old faces. But then again, there's something reassuring about it as well.

ELEVEN

SPARE PARTS:
A BRIEF MISCELLANY

I'll keep it short, but if you do any of your own bike maintenance, you'll know what I'm talking about: you soon accumulate a ragbag of odds and ends at the bottom of your toolbox – spare parts, links of chain, assorted washers, nuts and bolts. I never want to throw anything away, just because you never know when you'll strip the thread of a vital bolt, need a make-do replacement, and find the idea of making a trip to a bike shop to buy one utterly unbearable. So you end up with buckets of bike bits, with the satisfying heft of a jar-full of pennies – but rather less value.

That just about sums up what we have here: occasional pieces, which may once have had a specific use and purpose, but are now just rattling around in the forlorn hope that someone may find another use for them one day and put them back on a bike. So this chapter is a kind of Frankenstein's monster of reassembled oddments, which probably merits an apology. Then again, you never know when you might find something that comes in handy. (For the record, I paused before including the Tyler Hamilton interview, and the subsequent story about his bizarre quest to challenge the scientific validity of the test that found him guilty of blood-doping. His racing career has since imploded further by his implication in the Spanish police's Operación Puerto enquiry into Dr Fuentes' doping ring. But I left these pieces in because this scenario is, unfortunately, a recurrent theme in professional cycling; so they stand as a kind of cautionary tale about how wary we should be of worshipping heroes in cycling.)

Tuesday November 22, 2005

EAT MY DUST

Don't be surprised to see the US president leading some of China's top mountain bikers trailing – Bush is the wheel deal, says Matt Seaton

The last time we heard about George W Bush and his mountain biking, there was a distinct whiff of schadenfreude in the air. He'd taken a tumble while riding round his ranch in Crawford, Texas, and had roughed himself up a bit. There were visible scrapes on his chin and nose for several days afterwards. For those who like to see the mighty brought low, there was a transitory poetic justice about Bush's fall.

However, like the good cowboy we know he is, the president was soon back in the saddle. And now he has taken time out from the busy schedule of his visit to China to hit the trail again: he was photographed on Sunday on his Trek, leading a posse of Lycra-clad Chinese Olympic hopefuls. So, not content with handing the Chinese government a stiff lecture on religious freedom, he gave their top mountain bikers a good kicking too.

Of course, seeing our leaders do a photo-op on a bike is not an entirely new phenomenon. Tony Blair has done it, and David Cameron has copied him. John Kerry is a keen cyclist, and Bill Clinton was a regular rider. But not many would travel with their bikes on foreign trips, let alone take a couple of hours out of a 36-hour top-level diplomatic initiative to go for a training session. I'm always telling people how easy it is to fly with a bike – easier than getting a bike on a train, in fact. I wonder if the president has a bike mechanic among his retinue? I dare say some of those secret-service guys are handy with a spanner.

Actually, I would not be surprised if the president could take care of things himself. What we learn from this picture of Bush on the trail in Beijing is that he's a pretty serious mountain biker. The bike is a carbon-fibre Trek, with Rock Shox front forks. Not totally top-end, but you get an awful lot of bike for $3,000 these days. He's wearing Sidi off-road shoes – $200 items designed for competition: light, stiff, with ski-binding-style cleats. Admittedly, the president's jacket and shorts are bulky and baggy, compared with the Chinese cyclists' more professional all-in-one Lycra suits. But, in fact, his style is mainstream for off-roaders, and, arguably, Bush wins brownie points for not wearing those wussy tights the Chinese team have on. Even the president of the United States must sometimes have to stand bare-legged.

The helmet is generic but late-model; the full-finger gloves are purpose-made; and the eyewear is sophisticated with lenses that enhance vision in low-light conditions. But the real give-away here is that his wristwatch is not a watch at all – it's a heartrate monitor (HRM). Now that's a real bike nut's piece of kit. What this means is that when Bush was packing his bags to go to China, he wasn't thinking about trade or Tibet. He was thinking: Jeez, three days without a workout … you know what, I'm going to take my bike – better take the HRM, too.

Last year, a journalist from Associated Press joined the president on a lap of his Crawford ranch. Bush's heart rate, Scott Lindlaw reported, peaked at 168 beats a minute during the 18-

mile loop. For a man of his age (59), that's likely to be about 95% of his maximum, which is the sort of intensity only elite athletes train at. According to AP, Bush completed the ride in an hour and 20 minutes. That's more than 13mph, which may not sound all that fast, but for an off-road cyclist, believe me, it's shifting. His resting pulse – a good rule-of-thumb indicator of fitness – is down in the 40s. On this form, Bush could not only hold his own in age-related cross-country races, he'd win some.

We have already heard from Sir Christopher Meyer's memoirs, DC Confidential, that intellectually Bush is not the lunk we took him for. But now we discover he's a kick-ass cyclist too. And that's a thoroughly dispiriting thought: not only does the most rightwing American president since, well, Ronald Reagan, clearly love cycling as much as I do, but he's a real bikie, not some loafing nodder. We always knew Bush spent an inordinate amount of time home on the range, but we just thought he was a bit workshy and easily bored with ruling the free world. It turns out he's been honing himself as a two-wheeled athlete.

The only compensation is that, according to AP, Bush barks when he's pedalling hard uphill, giving out a low growl with every stroke: "Hrrr, hrrr, hrrr"; a sort of simian male version of the Sharapova grunt. At least, if I went for a ride with the president, I could tease him about that. Not that I'd see him for dust, of course.

Saturday May 13, 2006

DAY 15,996: BIKE STOLEN IN PORTSMOUTH. DAY 16,000: NICE RIDE WITH NEWSPAPER CHAP

Round-the-world cyclist Heinz Stücke got his bicycle back this week. So our cycling columnist, Matt Seaton, caught up with him

Forty-four years on the road and a third of a million miles have given Heinz Stücke a philosophical cast of mind. Within hours of getting off the ferry from France in Portsmouth on Monday night, the bicycle that has been his constant companion since 1962 was stolen. But he's not bitter.

"I trust everybody," he says, "because if you didn't, you just wouldn't go around the world. You take a calculated risk all the time everywhere you go."

In fact, his bike – a unique artefact that already has a place booked for it in a museum of cycling back in Heinz's native Germany – was returned to him little more than 36 hours after its theft. After the story was picked up by the national media, the thief probably realised that Heinz's steed might be more trouble than it was worth.

When he meets me at Portsmouth harbour station, he and his bike attract a small crowd of curious wellwishers. We convoy through busy traffic to a quieter spot by the beach. His bulky bike makes stately progress. When he signals to change lane, Heinz has the air of a benevolent if diminutive emperor: a lord of the open road.

In the course of amassing his world-beating tally of 211 countries and territories, Heinz has seen it all before. This is not the first time his bike has been stolen; it's the sixth. "The last time was in 1997 – almost every 10 years it's been stolen. That's not bad in 150,000km."

The last occasion was in Siberia, in a town about 600 miles east of lake Baikal. Then, too, local media got involved and his bike and luggage were soon recovered. One item not returned was his belt, so a Russian police officer gave him hers – one of many mementoes from his 16,000 days on the road.

It all started in the small town of Hövelhof, Germany, in the late 1950s, when he was apprenticed as a tool- and die-maker. "I hated it every morning," he recalls. "I was 14 and getting up at 20 to six every morning to catch the train."

Travel offered an escape. But his experience in metallurgy has come in handy. His bike frame has been mended 16 times – looking closely, I can see how patched and dented it is under the black enamel and painted place names.

At one time, part of the tubing was rusting because of the sweat dripping off his nose. "I do believe there is nobody in this world who has sweated as much as I have," he jokes. "Probably half a gallon a day."

And there have been the inevitable crashes, especially every cyclist's nightmare – the car door opening. But with a bike weighing 25kg (about 4st), loaded with another 40-50kg of luggage, Heinz says the car doors tend to come off worse. My lightweight racer looks positively puny next to his tank, yet he pilots it past the lunchtime joggers on the harbourside with an easy grace. He only doesn't like riding in the rain, he says – it gives him a skin rash.

He has encountered more exotic hazards – twice attacked and severely injured by swarms of bees in Africa. Perhaps his closest shave came in Zambia in 1980, when, near the border with the newly independent Zimbabwe, he ran into some disgruntled former fighters from Joshua Nkomo's Zapu guerrilla army.

"I saw armed people walking on the road. They saw me coming and stopped me. One put his hand here on my handle-bars. I said I was a tourist from Germany, and I moved to get my passport. Maybe he thought I was going to get my gun ..."

The bike toppled over and Heinz jumped clear.

"I said, 'What do you want?' And he shot at me, just like that. I didn't even know the bullet had gone through my big toe. There was no pain or anything. But then they all closed in on me."

It was only when they took his shoes that he realised he was bleeding from the wound. Then he was pushed into a ditch at the side of the road. Did he think the end had come?

"I had no idea. At that time, there was no thinking, no anything. All I was trying to do was not provoke them in any way."

He was rescued after a passing German aid worker raised the alarm with the Zambian police. Fortunately, the bullet had just grazed the bone.

These days, he chiefly earns the money to finance his travels by selling an illustrated booklet about his experiences. He just sets his bike on its stand and that's his pitch. He is constantly meeting people yet it's a solitary road he travels. Is he never lonely?

"You need female companionship sometimes, but this is another person. And that's too bad because you have to deal with another person."

In any case, he is not much of a catch these days, he says with a chuckle: "I've had many little affairs. Now, it's more complicated: I'm 66, and on a bicycle, and I sleep in a tent ...

"The only woman I knew for a long time was my Russian girlfriend [Zoya], for eight years. Until one time I came back from a trip around the Caribbean, I called her and she said, 'I'm married now.' Just like that. I didn't want to believe it really.

"But you have to understand her, as well, because a woman wants maybe more companionship than just every few months."

Did he ever imagine when he set out, 44 years ago, that he would be on the road all this time?

"Nobody knows that far ahead. Ten years into the journey, it was 'I don't want to go back to the factory'. But then it just becomes such a part of you."

The freedom of travel is something many people crave – one reason they love his story and buy his brochure. But, he says, it takes special commitment.

"That dream is for everybody all the time, but unfortunately it can't be easily realised. You really have to cut all your relations, family, and be free. You have some saved-up money for a year or two, and then you have to find new money. Eventually, people wind up again where they started from. Or they get a good job somewhere else. And then the woman comes, you know. And then they buy a house and then, maybe, children come.

"And then only the dream stays."

And with that, he pedals on his way.

Monday June 12, 2006

At 3pm on Saturday afternoon most of London was congregated in pubs and living rooms watching England's opening World Cup match against Paraguay. But several hundred people were gathering at Hyde Park Corner for a spectacle of a very different sort: a naked bike ride.

June 10 was London's second annual World Naked Bike Ride, a new kind of pro-bike protest against global warming and the oil business. A bit like Critical Mass, but without the clothes. According to the event's website, full nudity is not compulsory – "as bare as you dare" is the ethos – but plenty of people seemed to be taking up the challenge.

Cyclists of both sexes, all ages and every conceivable shape and size could be seen in various states of disrobement. Some were keeping a few items of clothing on until the last minute, but many had already thrown caution to the wind (along with their underwear) and were busy applying sunscreen to parts not normally on view half a mile from Buckingham Palace.

A score of bike-mounted police officers were on hand, not to arrest nude cyclists for outraging public decency, but to escort the ride through the streets on its five-mile tour of the capital. Frankly, with their DayGlo vests and black jumpsuits, they looked a bit overdressed.

A few minutes before departure, bemused onlookers were treated to the sight of the Household Cavalry, the sunlight glinting off their breastplates, riding through Wellington Arch and past massed ranks of completely starkers cyclists. Only in England.

It was certainly picturesque and probably great for tourism, but besides that, what is the point of a naked bike ride?

"The longer I live in London, the more I think it needs to become a bike metropolis," said Claire, a woman in her 30s on a mountain bike, "and this is a very pointed way of making that message heard."

So is the nudity thing just a stunt then, I asked Mark, who was wearing leopard-print bodypaint and very little else. "It's about saying that we're a vulnerable species on the road."

But for Maggie, an American living in London, there was a more positive message. "It's also about demonstrating the muscle of cycle power as an alternative to oil dependency."

Inspector Neil Ascherson was conducting the police escort operation. Unlike most of his officers, he was sporting a rather natty pair of shorts and showing a bit of leg. Didn't he feel like getting more into the spirit of the thing?

"Being in a disciplined organisation, we do have to adhere to a dress code and that's what we're going to stick to, I'm afraid – much as we may be tempted in this lovely weather."

Venus (her real name) is a veteran of the Naked Bike Ride. Last year, when the ride attracted about 250 cyclists, her slogan as she rode past the US embassy was "My bush for president". Apparently, she got some votes for that.

But the purpose of the Naked Bike Ride is not just protest. "A lot of people point the finger at George Bush and Tony Blair, but we're all responsible for climate change," she said. "So it would be nice if everyone made more of an effort to ride a bike instead of driving a car."

And many were making the effort. This year, the warm weather had brought out even more: 500 would be a conservative estimate. By the time the ride wound around Trafalgar Square, football fans were pouring out of bars. Some clearly wondered if the beer had been that strong.

Meanwhile, the open-top buses were giving sightseers an unexpected bonus. Camera-wielding tourists were frantically leaning over the sides to get a better angle.

Simon, on the ride for his first time, came along with some naturists who wished to publicise a favourite beach threatened by development. "My friends were here last year when it was 15 degrees, and they said it was very cold indeed – and that doesn't do many favours for a man."

Not a problem this year, with the thermometer nudging 30. But are there comfort issues, I wondered, with this naked riding lark? "Er, yes, my saddle's a bit narrow."

Ouch. But what struck me as strange as I pedalled along, still clothed and brandishing my microphone as a badge of professional office, was that I was the one who felt self-conscious and bashful. Perhaps this look – helmet and shoes, and nothing else – might catch on, I asked Maggie.

"Only in June."

Monday January 9, 2006

MAKING TRACKS

In some parts of Europe, a quarter of all journeys are made by bike. In Britain the figure is 2%. Can anything persuade us to leave our cars and get pedalling? Perhaps the unlikeliest of towns – Darlington – holds the key. Matt Seaton reports

It's a damp, chilly day in Darlington. Oli Lougheed assures me, a softy southerner up from London for the day, that it's not usually like this. Here, on the eastern side of the Pennines, he says, it may be cold in winter, but it's normally clear and dry. Lougheed is not, in fact, from the local tourist board, but he does work for Darlington. He is the town's cycling officer, and today he is showing me how the town is making itself more cycle-friendly. Which explains his anxiety about the grim weather: as we make our way from the station to the town centre, there are not many cyclists in evidence.

But then, there never are. Just 1% of all journeys in Darlington are made by bicycle. As Lougheed says, almost cheerfully, "You can't really go much lower than that."

The national average is 2% "modal share", as they say in the jargon of transport professionals, meaning that 2% of all journeys are made by bike. A few towns, such as Cambridge, York and Richmond-upon-Thames, where, historically, cycling has been popular and local authorities progressive, have much higher numbers. But they are notable exceptions. Even in gridlocked London, despite impressive recent improvements in the centre of the city, the national figure of 2% applies.

The reason Lougheed is actually quite chipper about his job is that Darlington recently became one of six towns in Britain to be selected as a "cycling demonstration town", designed to set an example in how to transform urban sprawls into two-wheeled havens (the others are Aylesbury, Brighton, Derby, Exeter and Lancaster). Under this scheme, part-funded by the Department for Transport (DfT) with matching cash from each local authority, the towns will get £1m a year for three years, all to be spent on promoting cycle use. If there's any way that cycling can be made a serious part of Britain's transport policy, Darlington, it's hoped, will be the place to find it.

Lougheed's usual share of the annual transport budget would be £150,000, which is not nothing: for £3,000, for instance, he could put 30 schoolchildren through a 10-week cycle training course. But when you consider that a single cycle lane can cost £60,000 a mile to build, you begin to see what Lougheed is up against with his 1% modal share – and what a boon this new award will be.

Cycling England is the body behind the scheme. The successor to the purely advisory National Cycling Strategy Board, it was launched earlier this year as a revamped executive body with spending powers. Initially, it hoped to have a budget of £70m – which would have represented just over 1.5% of the Department for Transport's gargantuan £4.1bn annual budget. But with the Treasury putting the screws on government departments last year, this was slashed. In the end, Cycling England was given just £5m a year for three years (about 0.1% of the DfT budget).

One of its board members is John Grimshaw, chief executive of Sustrans, the voluntary organisation behind the remarkably successful National Cycle Network (NCN). He is under no illusions about the uphill task Cycling England faces. While the equivalent town in Denmark might have 25% of trips made by bike, cycle use in Darlington is almost nonexistent.

"What we would like to get out of the cycle demonstration town project," says Phillip Darnton, chair of Cycling England

(and a former managing director at Raleigh), "is the clearest possible indication that investing at European levels will make a real difference to the number of trips people make by bike." Promoting cycling, he says, is too dependent on local, sometimes individual, political backing. "At the moment, it is a matter of political will; until it becomes a matter of policy, results will be very spotty."

The government has slowly increased spending over the past seven or eight years, from approximately 60p per head of population to 80p. But this compares with £5-£18 per capita in other parts of Europe – and those levels have been sustained for a decade or more. Under the demonstration scheme, towns such as Darlington are getting funding that works out at about £5 per head of population – at the lower end of the European scale, but still a massive increase on the national average.

So how exactly does a town go about making itself cycle-friendly? What does that fiver a head buy?

The problem for Darlington is that it starts from such a low level that the most basic groundwork is still to be done. The borough has a population of 98,000 people, 85% of whom live in the urban area. Historically, Darlington was a market town, situated between the Yorkshire Dales to the west and Middlesbrough and the coast to the east. Unlike many parts of the north-east, it was not dependent on coalmining or heavy industry, so survived deindustrialisation better than most. Its heyday came in the 19th century with the railways – the first passenger railway in the land ran from Stockton to Darlington. The town's status as a transport hub (the A1 passes right by Darlington, as well as the East Coast mainline through it) has provided employment ever since.

Darlington is no more than four miles wide on its longest axis (east-west): you could cycle end to end in 15 minutes.

From the outskirts to the inner pedestrian precinct could never be more than a couple of miles, but 80% of car trips are into the city centre. The transport unit's research shows that 34% of car journeys could, theoretically, be done by bike (short trips with no passengers or loads).

The sorry history of cycle use in Darlington is one of low investment and poor infrastructure. There were some cycle routes but, says Lougheed, "They were a classic case of good idea in theory, but which took you nowhere, so that you end up thinking [they] may as well not have been built."

Cyclists are all too familiar with the bad old bike routes – the ones that seemed like a particularly unfunny practical joke by some disgruntled traffic engineer. The problem of idiotic cycle lanes has had a doubly unfortunate effect: because they're badly designed, cyclists don't use them, but then councillors ask transport officers why on earth they should fund more when the ones they already have don't get used. "We're paying heavily for bad infrastructure," agrees Phillip Darnton, of Cycling England.

Under the new scheme, Darlington's transport team plans to put in nine or 10 "radial routes", running from the periphery right to the centre. The problem with Darlington, explains Darnton, is that it's a perfect example of old-school town planning – a pedestrianised centre (which excludes cyclists), surrounded by an inner ring road that is a busy dual carriageway (presenting a formidable obstacle to pedestrians and cyclists alike). The new radial routes will reassign priorities where they intersect the ring road, and will make all the formerly pedestrianised areas dual use. The philosophy here is that cyclists can coexist perfectly safely with walkers, European-style; where it is clear that an area is dual use, cyclists automatically adjust their behaviour, slowing down and riding sensibly. In addition, there will be more parking, including secure lockers in the town centre car parks.

"The object is to create boulevards rather than traffic corridors," says Tim Crawshaw, the council's chief designer of the public environment. He admits that part of the aim is to make Darlington "more prosperous" as well as a better place to live.

You can see the vision here: Darlington's population, mainly employed in the service sector, will be cycling and walking around the town, enjoying a new cafe society and lively street life. The object is to turn Darlington into an Amsterdam or Utrecht of northern England. But what about the weather? Wouldn't today's freezing fog put off these putative new cyclists?

"Look at Stockholm," Lougheed replies. "It's colder there, and rains more, but cycling there has a 15% modal share. That instantly ends the argument." But would a figure like that really be achievable in Darlington? Not any time soon. "The difficult thing is that you build the infrastructure and promote it," says Lougheed, "but it takes years for people to change their habits." Their target is a much more modest 3% – a threefold increase – by 2011.

The bulk of the spending will go on hardware (lanes, signs, crossings, etc), with £500,000 for marketing. But it's not just a question of printing up leaflets and getting a photo-op in the local paper. Under the scheme, Lougheed is hiring a highway engineer specifically to oversee the new cycling infrastructure. Teams of people will go around each locality in turn, knocking on doors, distributing maps of cycle routes and talking to people, offering a consultation that can lead to advice and training, even discounts at local bike shops. They get a 40% take-up of these one-on-one consultations – "It's the biggest thing for making a quick difference," says Lougheed.

One thing that has already changed is that there are now more people in the policy team who cycle. "We walk the talk," says Tim Crawshaw proudly. "That's a very strong message."

All this is part of a quiet revolution under way not only in Darlington, but all over the country. The hierarchy of road users that transport officers such as Lougheed now work with reads as follows: disabled and visually impaired people first, pedestrians next, then cyclists, public transport, delivery vehicles, cars used for business with more than one occupant and, at the bottom of the heap, single-occupancy motorists. This is the new orthodoxy in local transport planning, though it requires a huge shift in mindset among planners and highway engineers.

Much of this change comes under the banner of road safety – hence, for example, the growth of 20mph zones in built-up areas. But there is also a wealth of other psychological tricks in the traffic engineer's armoury. As I cycle down a broad residential street with Lougheed, he tells me how a simple measure such as taking out the central white line will reduce traffic speeds. Without the sense of a safe, segregated corridor down which they can drive at 35mph, motorists instinctively move towards the middle of the road. But then they become aware of needing to drive more slowly in case they meet a car coming the other way. All of a sudden, they're driving at 25mph – just because a white line has been taken out. Lougheed points out that very often urban areas are so congested that "slower speeds actually improve traffic flows".

"Drive slower, get there faster" may be a tough message to sell. Research shows that drivers habitually underestimate the length of time a given journey will take by as much as 50%. And ask the same person how long a journey by bicycle will take, typically they will overestimate by the same factor. Turning round that mentality is a huge challenge. "It's about creating a culture of cycling," says Lougheed.

Transport planners in London have found the same thing: that it can be something intangible in the air that is the most convincing factor in persuading people to get on their bikes. London has become the flagship for the cycling lobby: earlier this year the mayor, Ken Livingstone, announced that cycle use had doubled in the capital since 2000, which meant that Transport for London's target of an 80% increase by 2010 had already been more than met, five years early. All sorts of changes have helped deliver this: in the past two years, for instance, London boroughs have put in 5,000 parking stands; most junctions now have advance stop lines; more and more schools are getting their bike sheds back. The level of spending has steadily risen, and now stands at £20m a year. But as Rose Ades, head of TfL's cycling policy unit, puts it, "It's not just cycle lanes, it's a whole package of measures" – the key being that "you have to get in the air a sense of confidence about cycling".

According to Lougheed, the magic number for cycle use is 4% of all journeys made by bike. This is a classic "tipping point", the term popularised by the American journalist Malcolm Gladwell, in his book of the same name. For a tipping point to be achieved, an idea about the desirability of a particular product or behaviour or lifestyle choice has to work its way into the public consciousness like a virus until it reaches a critical mass. What everyone in the cycling lobby is talking about is the need to plant a cycling meme, "infecting" the population with the notion that maybe it would be quite convenient, even pleasant, to cycle instead of drive. Cultural change is something you catch off other people.

"You get to 4% and, on any trip in a car, you see a cyclist," says Lougheed. "Drivers start to use the left-hand mirror more. They get used to cyclists being part of the traffic. And cycling becomes a stronger part of street culture and fashion. It's seen as cool."

Can cycling really be cool in Darlington? Lougheed is confident. "Other places that have used the same plan with less investment and fewer staff have succeeded. By that logic, we can't fail." "If you go back to the 80s in Germany," says John Grimshaw, "they spent the money and they got serious increases in cycling, which they managed to sustain."

Darlington, then, is the crucible of a grand experiment. There's a lot riding on it. "If we're wrong," says Darnton, "we've blown it completely".

Monday June 28, 2004

Tyler Hamilton arrives for a late lunch at a hotel in his European home of Girona looking as if he scarcely broke sweat during a 90-mile training ride in the foothills of the Pyrenees. The only sign of his morning's exertions is that he has caught some Spanish sun; a native of New England, Hamilton has fair, freckled skin. The initial impression he makes is one of slightness, even frailty.

It is easy to forget, until one gets up close, that most top cyclists have the physiques of jockeys or bantamweight boxers. In a long stage race such as the Tour de France, which starts on Saturday, the game is ultimately decided by who can prevail in the high mountains. That makes power-to-weight the crucial formula. With his slender arms, skinny torso and sculpted legs, Hamilton is typical in the pro peloton.

was that we rode as a cohesive unit – not necessarily that we won but that we were the strongest team in the race, for sure."

While this might sound like standard "team leader talking up prospects" stuff, following Phonak's subsequent results has been instructive. In June's week-long Dauphiné Libéré stage race, traditionally used as a pre-Tour warm-up by the favourites, Hamilton came second behind the Spanish climbing ace Iban Mayo. Armstrong was fourth behind Hamilton's team-mate Oscar Sevilla. And Hamilton had said he was going to use the Dauphiné for "training" only.

Still more significantly, given that one of the decisive stages in this year's Tour de France will be a time-trial (individual race against the clock) up the Alpe d'Huez, the Dauphiné included a trial to the top of Provence's daunting Mont Ventoux. Phonak placed five men in the top 15. In recent Tours what Armstrong calls the "blue train" of his US Postal squad has dictated the race in the mountains. This year a rather lurid green-and-yellow version may be much in evidence.

"Taking out a flat time-trial and adding a mountain time-trial is a big advantage to guys like Mayo, [Ivan] Basso, [Roberto] Heras," Hamilton forecasts, "because the strong time-triallists are not going to put two, three minutes into those guys. This year's Tour suits more of a pure climber than in the past. It'll be a more open Tour than for some time."

So could it be Hamilton's year?

"I think I have a chance," he says. "There's Lance, there's [Jan] Ullrich, there are many others who are big contenders. For me, I think I need to ride a perfect race. Lance last year, he didn't ride a perfect race and he still won."

It may be an open race but how clean will it be? As a distinctly testy note crept into Hamilton's voice when asked about his reasons for switching from CSC to Phonak, the subject of drugs is not easily raised. It is not, generally, a professional cyclist's favourite topic for small talk. But Hamilton is unexpectedly forthcoming.

"I think it's in a good phase," he says. "I can't speak for the other teams but I can speak for my team and myself. I feel like it's cleaned up a lot. I got tested three times in the off-season; that's just out-of-competition testing. And with all three teams I've been on I've signed my contract knowing if I use illegal substances I'm fired straight away.

"I think it's getting better, though there is a lot of silence. But maybe the teams aren't so open because of the journalists. If they don't always write the truth, and then someone like [the retired Kelme rider Jesus] Manzano speaks, they take it word for word as though it's the truth. Between him and [the former Cofidis professional Philippe] Gaumont, they've done so much damage to the sport, and how do we know it's all true?"

In fact, Gaumont's testimony – that his Scottish team-mate David Millar had supplied him with erythropoietin (the blood-doping agent EPO) during last year's Tour – appears reliable given the report in Friday's edition of L'Equipe that, during questioning by French police, Millar allegedly admitted EPO use. Part of the solution to cycling's perennial dope problem, Hamilton believes, could be to establish a riders' union to look after cyclists' interests, including their long-term health. "Right now I don't have much time to focus on something like that but maybe after my career is over it will be something I could try to help out with – to rally the troops."

Though his boyish, almost baby-faced looks belie it, at 33 the clock is running for Hamilton. He feels, though, that his best is yet to come.

"As long as I'm enjoying it, feeling like I'm still improving, and have the passion for it, I want to continue. I'm never satisfied. I always want to achieve more. I think Lance has that in him, the same dedication to being perfect, to riding the best race. That's the fire inside me."

Thursday June 23, 2005

Next month should see the conclusion of one of the most bizarre and intriguing legal challenges ever mounted by an athlete to a doping ban. Weeks after he won gold in the time trial at last summer's Athens Olympics, the US cyclist Tyler Hamilton failed a new blood test. Hamilton has fought the findings of the test ever since. His appeal against the two-year ban imposed by the United States anti-doping agency is due to be heard in July.

Blood-doping has long been popular in extreme endurance sports. If an athlete can boost the number of red blood cells, this improves the efficiency of the oxygen transport system. In the 1990s, performance hikes of 10-20% were made possible by a drug originally developed for kidney dialysis patients, erythropoietin (EPO), which stimulates the bone marrow to produce more red cells.

By 2000, a test for EPO became available, seeming to close the door on this type of doping. However, it remained possible to have a transfusion either of an athlete's own stored blood or someone else's. The latter is what Hamilton is presumed to have done, as he fell foul of the new test designed to detect mixed blood.

Protestations of innocence by athletes caught cheating are common, but rarely is the scientific validity of a test challenged. Yet this is what Hamilton has set about, mounting a legal challenge to the doping agency that has already cost several hundred thousand dollars.

Hamilton lost the first round at an arbitration court and received a two-year ban (which would, at the age of 34, in effect end his career). But he was encouraged by the fact that the three-person panel was split. The dissenting member, a former wrestler named Christopher Campbell, issued a strongly worded critique of the test.

Hamilton's key argument, highlighted by Campbell's statement, is that no rate of false positives has been determined for the new test.

"I think it's very unlikely they would be using a test without a known false positive rate," says Richard Budgett, chief medical officer of the British Olympic Association. Yet this is exactly what Hamilton's team says occurred.

But this raises the question of how, if not through transfusion, could someone have mixed blood populations?

There are other possible physiological causes, but two can be ruled out immediately for an elite athlete in peak condition: disease (some cancers can produce mixed blood populations) and bone marrow transplantation. That would leave two theoretical options: intra-uterine twin transfusion, and human chimerism.

Here we enter a twilight zone of biological oddity. The first theory relies on the notion of the "vanishing twin" syndrome – a twin pregnancy where one embryo fails to develop and is ultimately absorbed into the other, but leaves a phantom of its DNA in its surviving twin. It is impossible, however, to discover how often this results in the "microchimerism" of an adult still showing trace blood cells with a vanished twin's DNA.

The alternative proposal – that a person might be a human chimera, naturally producing more than one person's blood groups – is essentially the same theory but without the long-lost sibling. According to a recently published paper, this is common in women who have had children.

Hamilton, of course, has never been pregnant, and chimerism is extremely rare. According to one source, only 45 cases have been recorded. This may be because no one has gone looking for it, although a 1996 Danish study found blood chimerism in 8% of fraternal twins (and 21% of fraternal triplets). According to the New York Times, Ann Reed, a research director at the Mayo Clinic in the US, has found that 50-70% of people exhibit chimerism, or "genetic mosaicism".

In the absence of definitive data, the chimerism hypothesis was not offered as part of Hamilton's defence. But its mere possibility did open a chink in the prosecution case, the theoretical chance that something other than a transfusion could be to blame. Blood chimerism could give a false positive result in a test devised to detect someone else's cells.

When establishing a new scientific test, two protocols are regarded as axiomatic: submission to peer review and determination of the rate of false positives. Validation of the test that snared Hamilton is central to his case.

"Very few tests are 100% sensitive and specific," says Roger Palfreeman, the doctor for the British cycling team. "In any validation study, you would mention and work out the rates for true and false positives and negatives. Ideally, to obtain a true value, it should be done on a large enough population. A small sample size will give only an estimate of what would occur in a population."

"Most of these tests are extremely reliable," says Budgett. "There are quite a few tests in the pipeline – there's one for human growth hormone, for instance – but one reason why they are delayed is so that it can be established that you don't get false positives or false negatives in different populations."

By coincidence, Hamilton too notes (on his website) that the test for human growth hormone has been delayed precisely because of the difficulties of validation.

So was the blood test sufficiently trialled? Asked whether it may have been rushed to market prematurely, as Hamilton implies, one expert commentator who did not wish to be identified says: "Possibly it was hurried through in time for Athens."

Budgett remains sanguine. "People have long arguments about whether the standard of proof in these tests should be 'beyond reasonable doubt' or 'on the balance of probability'. The consensus is that it should lie somewhere between."

Hamilton's challenge may have revealed an element of reasonable doubt, but will he succeed in tipping the balance of probability? If he does, then the entire anti-doping establishment will be forced to admit that it gambled its credibility on a bad bet.

from Rouleur, vol.1, 2005

FIXED IDEA

"I still feel that variable gears are only for people over 45. Isn't it better to triumph by the strength of your muscles than by the artifice of a derailleur?" asked Henri Desgrange in 1902. It was still a year before he founded the Tour de France as a promotion for the sports newspaper he edited (L'Auto, which later became L'Equipe), but Desgrange never lost his prejudice against bikes with gears. "We are getting soft," he scorned, and in 1912 he tried to ban Tour riders even from using a freewheel mechanism on their single-speed machines – two years after he had sent the Tour into the high mountains for the first time. As if the menace of the bears and bandits that roamed the slopes of the Pyrenees was not enough, imagine having to ride it on a fixed gear. (And which would be worse: going up or down?)

It was not until 1936, as illness finally forced the ageing Desgrange to relax the iron grip in which he had held the event for more than three decades, that the Tour permitted riders the luxury of using multiple gears. Even then, Desgrange's successor, Jacques Goddet, fined one rider a 10-minute penalty for anticipating the rule change, which was not officially confirmed until the 1937 Tour.

So it was that Maurice Garin won the first Tour de France in 1903 on a fixed-gear bicycle that differed only in avoirdupoids but not in its essentials from a fixed bike you would ride today. That historical resonance and the sense of fellowship become only deeper when you consider that Garin's average speed of nearly 16mph, sustained over three weeks and more than 1,500 miles, is a remarkable achievement on a fixed – especially one which weighed a fair few pounds more than a bike of modern manufacture. Only one rider in that first Tour of 1903 used a bike with a freewheel, Pierre Desvages; despite his BSA-made mechanism, he finished 20th. Instead, most riders eventually preferred to use a double-sided hub, and change their fixed-gear ratio by hopping off the bike when they reached a climb and turning the wheel round to use a larger sprocket. The timing of these enforced roadside pit-stops naturally became a highly tactical affair. It was not unknown for riders to bluff a gear change by flipping their wheel twice and remount in the same high gear, having fooled their rivals into switching to a low gear.

Prewar road races among the amateur ranks tended to be divided between fixed and freewheel events. A mixed bunch was considered dangerous because riders on fixed-gear bikes were forced to corner in a more conservative fashion than those with freewheels, with the risk of pedal-strike. Derailleurs, in any case, were frowned upon: all very well for tourists and vicars, but not for serious racers. "As for me, give me a fixed gear!" declaimed Desgrange. The editor of L'Auto was, notoriously, a pitiless martinet, a man more admired than liked, but in this emotion I match him wheel for wheel. Look around the city streets today and it is hard to spot a courier who does not ride a fixed. With ever more commuters emulating the messengers, you might be forgiven for thinking that the fixed-gear bike is an idea whose time has come. The truth is, it is an idea whose time has never gone. To ride a fixed-gear bike is to feel that your bike, and not just your bike but your whole experience as a rider, runs back through time as a strand of DNA that connects you with the original essence of cycling. Before multiple gears, before the freewheel, there was direct drive: the fixed gear.

The first great era of cycle sport belonged to the velodrome, on track bikes. This was the arena of Henri Desgrange himself, a former track professional, and of Major Taylor, the first African-American world champion in any sport. The end of the 19th century saw cycling attract huge crowds, of which the winter six-day events in Europe now are merely the echo. Cyclists on track bikes performed extraordinary feats of endurance, racing for 24 hours at a stretch, often on temporarily assembled wooden-boarded ovals. The ghosts of those early cycling heroes are still with us when we watch the bewildering choreography of "the Madison" at Olympics and world championships today: the event owes its name to the paired-rider races held at Madison Square Garden in New York. When you ride a fixed, you make that memory incarnate. To swing your leg over the top tube of a "fixie" is to pay homage to the fact that once, all bikes were this way.

I can't be sure whether I found my fixed, or whether my fixed found me. When I raced in my 20s, I used to own a cobbled-together track bike, which I kept stabled at Herne Hill velodrome. But when I gave up riding for several years, I told friends who were still racing that they could borrow it or cannibalise it for their own needs. So when I came back to cycling a couple of years ago, it was hardly surprising there was no trace of it at the velodrome. I searched in the cargo containers that serve as sheds there, but there was not even a rusty frame I could claim. I wanted to replace that bike with a bike I could ride on the track, but I also knew that I wanted a bike I could ride on the road as a fixed. I couldn't spend serious money on a new bike. For one thing, I wasn't even sure I was getting started again, or how much time I would have to ride. So, for some months, the fixed remained a fantasy, that back-of-the-mind wishful thinking where all new bikes begin.

Then, one Saturday, I was driving up the Brixton Road to take my daughter to her gymnastics club in Dulwich, London. I turned a corner off the main road to take advantage of a familiar rat-run, and something caught my eye in a shop window. It was one of those rather dubious retail establishments that sometimes seemed to sell second-hand bikes, mainly kids' bikes, and sometimes oddments of furniture from house clearances. More recently, it has mutated again, into that south London staple: the one-stop tyre shop. I dropped my daughter off at her class, and 15 minutes later I was pulling up outside the shop. There it was: a blue and orange Condor Cycles frame with track ends, Ambrosio A8 carbon forks, a single front brake – and a rear wheel with a double-sided hub, fixed on one side, single-speed freewheel on the other. It looked laughably out of place amid the detritus of low-end, recycled Halfords stock. I could hardly contain my excitement. My heartrate was hitting zone 4, just standing there. It was so exactly what I'd been looking for; I felt in some profound way it already had my name on it. I didn't even need to ask for a test ride. Just a quick glance told me that it was my size, or close enough. I just asked how much, and then ran over to the cashpoint at the petrol station across the road for a bunch of 20s.

Of course, I felt a twinge of guilt. I guessed it had very likely been a courier's bike, and I knew how likely it was that someone had come out of a building from making a drop and had been winded by that sick-to-the-stomach feeling of finding nothing but thin air where he had left his bike outside. I asked the man in the shop cautiously about the bike's provenance. He wasn't surprised or offended, but insisted it was legit and made me out a receipt. I took this gratefully as a figleaf for my conscience, but wondering if you can still be prosecuted for receiving stolen goods if you've actually got a receipt. I'm sure the answer is you can. When I told the story to a friend at Herne Hill, he laughed and said he knew the shop. Apparently, one day the sheds at the velodrome had been broken into and the entire stock of rental track bikes had disappeared on the back of a lorry. Within days, someone who worked at the track spotted the lot racked up and hanging on every wall in a second-hand shop. The police were called and the return of the bikes was swiftly negotiated. It was my second-hand shop, of course, the one on Brixton Road where I'd bought my much-dreamed-of fixed. I quickly spent as much again on my bike as I'd bought it for, changing the Stronglight chainset for a handsome Miche Primato, proper track wheels for riding at Herne Hill, a decent saddle and track bars. I rode the bike all summer, on road, on the track, around town. Although I reasoned that it was no longer quite the same bike as I'd bought, with my various improvements, for weeks I lived in dread of someone yelling at me in the street, "That's my bike you've got there." But in time the anxiety faded, and sheer pleasure took its place. No longer a mere initiate, I was a convert to the way of the fixed.

Riding a fixed is a powerfully sensual experience. The effect of the fixed gear is that the pedals are forced to revolve whenever the bicycle is in motion, as much by the momentum of bike and rider as by any force applied by the cyclist to the pedals. Instead of the bike seeming merely an inanimate tool that the cyclist puts to work, the fixed-gear bicycle asserts itself as something like a partner. The fixed gives you constant, rich feedback about your speed, the gradient, your cadence, the wind, the state of the road, the condition of your legs. It demands dialogue; it forces its point of view on your attention. To ride a fixed is to find yourself in a deeper relationship with a bike than anything you have hitherto realised. It is as if it has a mind of its own. You must treat it with respect and tact. If you do, then it will reward you with the smoothest, most comfortable, most subtly satisfying miles you will ever ride. If you choose a sensible gear, then you will roll as if there were always a gentle tailwind at your back. The miraculous sensation, transmitted through the cranks, that the bike "wants" to keep moving forward, that it is willing to work with you, somehow plants the idea that this is a perpetual motion machine, devised just for you. This is not entirely fanciful. The chain drive is a highly efficient transmission. With a well-maintained chain, friction losses can be as low as 1.5%. Which, put another way, means that the efficiency ratio of "power in" to "power out" can be as high as

98%. (Compare this with a car gearbox, which typically operates at about 85%.) Even the best derailleur mech will cost another 4-5% in friction losses. There is sound sense, as well as sensuousness, built into the simplicity of the fixed gear.

But it is the subjective quality of the ride that fixed aficionados love above all. There is a meditative, Zen-like quality to riding a fixed. More than ever, you are intimately aware of your cadence, the relationship between leg speed and ground speed. And yet it is an awareness just below the surface of consciousness, at that higher level of semi-reflexive motor function that seems to apply to many repeated, rhythmic physical actions. Pedalling a fixed has a lulling, soothing effect, which liberates your frontal lobes: your thoughts can go wherever they please. Riding a fixed can be mind-expanding business. You reach the end of your journey and find that you have solved some problem or made a resolution on the way, but without conscious effort. The fixed-gear bicycle has, of course, remained the staple of track cycling, where it is guaranteed that everyone is travelling in the same direction and, generally, at similar speeds. "No brakes" is the rule at the velodrome because, counter-intuitively, it is safer for no one to be able to stop suddenly.

The fixed for road use is often no more than a track bike with a front fork drilled for a single brake. The purist rides this way, with just one brake on the front; the theory being that the legs alone can provide sufficient braking on the rear wheel to make another brake redundant. And redundancy on a bicycle is, as we all know, chiefly an aesthetic crime. Others (myself included) prefer a belt-and-braces approach of two brakes and mudguards too. It is true that – around town, through traffic – riding a fixed encourages a steadier, more anticipatory mode of riding, which is arguably safer than the staccato, stop-start style of riding a bike with ordinary gears and brakes. Even so, for all-season riding, having the extra stopping power and the weather protection seems a modest but worthwhile abridgement of the fixed's purest form. It still feels like a fixed, even if it's not the thoroughbred of the species.

Professionals and coaches have long admired the effect that riding a fixed-gear bicycle has on a rider's pedalling style. The fixed has remained part of the pros' armoury, and has never really gone out of fashion. For them, the fixed is a training device, to be used in the off-season, to work on a strong but rounded pedal stroke and a fast, silky cadence. The fixed builds in strength training by forcing the rider to keep the gear turning when climbing a hill without being able to change down. Then, when descending, the rider is forced to spin the legs at very high revolutions without "bouncing" in the saddle. This, coaches have long held, promotes that wonderful but almost untranslatable French term "*souplesse*". According to Chris Carmichael, Lance Armstrong's longtime coach, the fixed is more efficient for winter training because it simply does not permit "coasting": "Because your legs are constantly in motion, this type of riding provides much more aerobic benefit than geared-bike riding. An hour and a half to two hours of fixed-gear riding is equivalent to four hours of regular riding."

Actually, you can coast on a fixed; it's just that your legs are still moving and you're not going very fast. But that, to me, is what makes the fixed an ideal bike for a recovery ride. An easy spin in not too long a gear feels like a massage. It promotes circulation, without too taxing an effort, and flushes away the toxins from sore muscles. More than any other bicycle, the fixed makes itself your friend and mentor. It works as your coach, improving your cycling and fitness, and it acts as your *soigneur*, taking care of your legs and ensuring that you listen to your body.

That fraternity or fellowship of the wheel that all cyclists at some level feel is redoubled for the "fixie". Sure, the fixed rider is a minority among a minority, an elite within an elite. More than that, though, fixies know that they share something essential and vital about the experience of cycling in its purest, highest form. What greater human bond can there be than to understand that someone else knows and feels exactly what you know and feel? And not just now, but down the generations of people who have got their kicks on bikes. That is why the fixed is not just a bike, even if it is the Ur-bike, a perfect machine. Beyond that, the fixed is a beautiful idea: *l'idée fixe.*

TWELVE

THE WRITE STUFF: ASSORTED BIKE LIT BITS

from Rapha (www.rapha.cc), October 2004

The Rider by Tim Krabbé, translated by Sam Garrett
  160pp, Bloomsbury, £6.99

Hovering ambiguously somewhere between memoir and fiction, The Rider is a purported account of a single bicycle race, the Tour de Mont Aigoual, set in the Cevennes region of south-west France. First published in its original Dutch edition in 1978, it was not translated into English for nearly a quarter of a century and then on the back of the novel of mystery and suspense for which Tim Krabbé is perhaps best known, The Vanishing – twice adapted for the big screen.

The Rider, though, is Krabbé's bestselling book back in his native Holland, and deservedly so. While his other fiction shows a superb command of narrative – few can match him for the virtuosity of his plot twists and tautness of his prose – there is a discursive, meditative quality to The Rider that makes it not just an account of a bike race but a metaphysical adventure. It is an existentialist novel in the grand European tradition of Camus and Beckett. Even the looming vistas of the Causses, the high plateaus through which the Tour winds, seem to echo the bleak landscape of the narrator's inner journey of exploration.

The Rider is peppered with anecdote and lore from the world of cycling, not drawn from recent history, of course, but concerning the heroes of the 50s, 60s and beyond. Stories that are not intended to be morally edifying or spiritually uplifting but that illustrate both the cruelty and strange camaraderie of cycle-racing. All of the key characters in The Rider – Barthélemy, Reilhan, Kléber, Lebusque, "the rider from Cycles Goff" and, above all, "Krabbé" himself – are tested in the crucible of this brutal bike race. The physical extremity of their privation and suffering as they battle it out in the mountains of the Cevennes can only be compared to men's experience of war. With typical economy, Krabbé composes an epic in less than 150 pages. It is a hymn to the human body, the realm of pure self-experience that only the true athlete knows.

The Rider is particularly acute at observing the grim tactical calculus that is a constant of any race: who has the best legs, which wheel to follow, when to attack? "Road racing imitates life," reflects the narrator, "the way it would be without the corruptive influence of civilisation. When you see an enemy lying on the ground, what's your first reaction? To help him to his feet. In road racing, you kick him to death."

But out of that ruthless evolutionary struggle something beautiful emerges. Like Roland Barthes, the French philosopher who wrote about the Tour de France as the perfect modern myth, Krabbé realised that the bicycle race has a natural narrative structure. If you have ever watched Jorgen Leth's classic film of the same era, A Sunday in Hell, a documentary about the Paris-Roubaix, you will appreciate the point. But better still, Krabbé dramatises the bike race and brings it to life.

He gives his characters a subjectivity that film can only hint at or hope for.

When you watch the Tour de France, so much is seen from the helicopter's point of view or, at best, from the back of a motorbike. Krabbé's haunting novella provides what no technology can: the intimacy of what it actually feels like to race. And more than that: what it really means.

Thursday October 9, 2003

Tim Krabbé's elegant, noirish novels are little known outside his native Holland. But the translation into English of The Vanishing is likely to change all that. He talks to Matt Seaton

"My last three novels, they were all about the same thing: the reunion in death of two lovers," says Tim Krabbé. Then he adds, with a rueful smile: "It's not a very light theme." But dark is what Krabbé does. In his fiction, at least. In person, he is a warm, engaging 60-year-old Dutchman: balding, with dark, bushy eyebrows, but tanned and physically vigorous. From his general demeanour you would think he had hit upon a way of bottling enthusiasm. Yet those of his novels published in English – The Cave, The Rider and now The Vanishing – have a contrastingly noirish sensibility, suggesting a brooding, melancholic imagination. The germ of a story, as in The Vanishing, might come from a newspaper clipping, but precisely where the wellspring of his fiction is to be found, Krabbé is not eager to speculate about.

"I'm always trying to stay naive about what's going on. I try only to be concerned with telling the story," he says. "If it's good, the depth will come all by itself."

Krabbé firmly resists the pigeonhole of thriller or mystery

writer and rightly so, for the literary finish and philosophical flavour of his work transcend the expectation-fulfilling formulae of genre fiction. He occupies similar literary territory to another recently reappraised writer, Patricia Highsmith. Like hers, his stories are tightly plotted, with strong characters and acute observation of social mores and individual psychology. But Krabbé's also have a more European, existentialist sense of the absurd – as if his characters dimly perceive themselves as victims of some bleak cosmic joke.

Krabbé's renaissance here is thanks largely to his publisher, Bloomsbury, which has teamed him with a gifted new translator, Sam Garrett, who has just won an award for doing full justice to Krabbé's lean, precise prose. To say that he was already one of Holland's best-known authors nevertheless sounds a little lame: to damn him with faint praise, perhaps. Given the context of an English linguistic imperialism that sees hundreds of British authors translated into Dutch every year, however, Krabbé's achievement as one of his country's few literary exports is considerable.

If Krabbé's name had any currency in the UK before now, it was as the author of the novel on which the films The Vanishing were based. "Films" plural because Krabbé's uncanny tale of a young woman's disappearance from a motorway service station and her boyfriend's obsessive search for her was adapted for the screen twice: first, in 1988, in a modest but memorable Dutch production, originally titled Spoorloos, that made a sufficient impression at the festivals to be dubbed in English and internationally distributed; then, in 1993, as a Hollywood remake, which – despite a promising cast including Jeff Bridges, Kiefer Sutherland and Sandra Bullock, and the same director – was "not so good", as Krabbé readily, if sardonically, observes.

Yet the book for which he is most renowned in his native Netherlands is De Renner, which came out in the UK last year as The Rider, a semi-autobiographical account of a bicycle race. Cycling is one of Krabbé's great enthusiasms. Though he came to it late, in his 30s, he became a keen amateur racer. Already a cult hit among the cycling cognoscenti here, The Rider has been so successful in Holland that last year, on the 25th anniversary of its Dutch publication, fans inaugurated a semi-competitive cycling tour through the south-west region of France that forms the backdrop to Krabbé's fictional race.

"Suffering always appealed to me – it's the essence of cycling," he explains. "When I was eight or nine, I loved running against my friends. I had an image of myself as able to endure physical strain."

As a boy, Krabbé was a good distance-runner and a keen footballer, as was his younger brother, despite being born into a highly artistic family. His father, like his father before him, was a painter – albeit not a very successful one. His parents divorced, unusually for the mid-50s, and his mother supported the family with her work as a children's author and translator who specialised in subtitling films. Thirteen at the time, Krabbé recalls his main emotion as "relief" – his relationship with his father was never an easy one, though he concedes that "he influenced me enormously". Somewhat bizarrely, his father, who was "aggressively non-conformist", stayed on in the family home, even after he had remarried. He is still alive and painting at 95; his mother died last year.

Krabbé grew up reading the novels of John O'Hara, Vladimir Nabokov and Graham Greene among others (he now admires Paul Auster), and knew that he wanted to be a writer early on, recalling, "the moment I decided, when I was 14". He published articles in his school magazine and has supported himself through his writing, living modestly, ever since.

Another possible career route was his other great passion: chess. "When I was 18, I dreamed of being a pro chess player," he says. As a young man in Amsterdam, he came close, dropping out of his degree in psychology. He reached the top 20 in Holland, but never the top 10: "I wasn't talented enough." It is one of Krabbé's traits – whether discussing the film version of The Vanishing or his merits as a chess player or cyclist – to be almost brutally realistic about his status. Perhaps there, in spite of his beguiling warmth and humour, you catch a glimpse of the novelist's cool, objectifying gaze.

A degree of ruthlessness is what you need as a cyclist and a chess player, of course, but Krabbé insists that, in both, it is as much the aesthetic dimension as the competitive one that compels him. He runs his own chess website, and composing problems – exercising what he calls "artistic chess" – still occupies much of his time. "It's like the joy you might feel at solving a mathematical puzzle: there might be some hidden, paradoxical, beautiful theme in there. I am very susceptible to this beauty."

So it is scarcely surprising that reviewers have often noted the spare, elegant architecture of his storytelling. "I often use it [composing chess problems] as a metaphor for writing, because when you're really in your book, nothing else matters. The beauty and force of what you're expressing is all you're interested in," he says, animatedly. "Truman Capote called it 'the secretary phenomenon' – as if the book were being dictated to you."

Krabbé presently has a busy few months ahead of him. His next novel, entitled Detours, has yet to finish being dictated to him. And he is getting married, for the second time, to Bernadette, a secondary-school teacher with a seven-year-old daughter. Krabbé has a 16-year-old son by his first wife: "It was not a good marriage," he says, but has proved a better friendship. In the meantime, Sam Garrett is busy translating two of Krabbé's books that are already published in Dutch: Delayed and Kathy's Daughter. The latter, says Krabbé, "is a very autobiographical story about a love affair with the daughter of someone I'd had a great love affair with when I was 19".

As ever, patterns and symmetries please him. Is this not, after all, another take on his "reunion of two lovers" theme? Not in death this time, perhaps. But, with Krabbé, you can be sure it won't be "light".

Saturday July 10, 2004

*Escaping from your parents or riding in the centenary Tour de France – Matt Seaton finds that cycling brings out the best in people in **Tim Hilton**'s One More Kilometre and We're in the Showers and **Matt Rendell**'s A Significant Other*

One More Kilometre and We're in the Showers: Memoirs of a Cyclist Tim Hilton, 410pp, HarperCollins, £16.99

A Significant Other: Riding the Centenary Tour de France with Lance Armstrong Matt Rendell, 182pp, Weidenfeld & Nicolson, £9.99

There have been some lean years in the literature of cycling – whole decades when the only intellectual sustenance for the hungry fan would be the slim volumes of autobiography by former professionals. These were, as a rule, scarcely literate, stuffed with cliche and chiefly comprising stories of outrageously self-justifying score-settling. Then came last year's rush to capitalise on the centenary of the Tour de France, creating an entire peloton of cycling books, of which one or two were excellent, some were good and a few can be quickly forgotten.

So it is pleasantly surprising to find that, with less haste and more loving care, the renaissance of cycling writing continues. One senses that, for Tim Hilton in particular, a former art critic both on this newspaper and the Independent on Sunday and author of an acclaimed biography of John Ruskin, there was suddenly a morning when he woke up and reflected that cycling might, after all, be a subject serious and worthy enough for literary endeavour. It is soon revealed that cycling has occupied a very central place in his life – certainly, I'd guess, as significant and intimate a place as art history and criticism. Cycling was Hilton's means of escape – from the claustrophobia of being an only child, the child moreover of communists.

To have communist parents in the 1940s was faintly exotic, but perhaps not as strange as it seems today. To be born into a "Party family", though, if not actually traumatic, was certainly an experience that set one apart. One feels for the young Tim, having to pass around the snacks as the comrades meet at his parents' house in Birmingham for their weekly discussion of dialectical materialism. No wonder he was soon off on his bike.

As Hilton quickly observes, however, it was largely to his egalitarian upbringing that he owed his affinity for cycling and his ability to make friends among the club-mates and people he met along the way. Artists rub shoulders with artisans in cycling's classless fellowship of the road – not forgetting, Hilton remarks, the strong representation of posties, whose habits of rising early and clocking off at lunchtime mesh perfectly with the requirement of amateur racing cyclists for "getting the miles in".

One More Kilometre is not simply a memoir: it is a deeply

affectionate mental scrapbook of cycling lore. Some has the flavour of very personal nostalgia – here is Hilton's memory of sleeping rough before an early-morning time trial: "I am old enough to remember the haystacks and still think it was a good way to spend a Saturday night." But much of the book consists of his impressions of the cycling heroes of the 40s, 50s and 60s, and their epic battles. In that respect, Hilton is typical of his generation: as he says, "All old wheelmen like such stories." The difference, of course, is that Hilton has the skill as a writer to make such well-worn subjects as the great postwar rivalry between the Italian duo Fausto Coppi and Gino Bartali fresh and compelling again.

And Hilton's breadth of knowledge and interest is considerable. How fascinating to discover, for instance, that Samuel Beckett's Waiting for Godot has a cycling connection. One Roger Godeau was a track ace at Paris's Vélodrome d'hiver after the war – this when the Vél d'hiv was still haunted by the fact that it had been used as a transit camp for 12,000 Jews, shamefully rounded up during the occupation by the French police. From that detention, they were transported to Drancy and thence to Auschwitz. In the late 40s, some of the boys who hung around the stadium for a sight of their cycling heroes told Beckett one day: *"On attend Godeau."* So Beckett perhaps had this melancholy setting, not to mention the shadow of the Holocaust, in mind when he was scripting the lines of Vladimir and Estragon.

Still, as a former member of "the Party" myself, I enjoyed most what was idiosyncratically Hilton's own story. He recalls with real feeling his relationship with the daughter of the celebrated communist historian Christopher Hill. Fanny Hill – as she was mischievously named by her father, after the heroine of John Cleland's then almost-unknown novella, Memoirs of a

Woman of Pleasure – had no particular interest in cycle racing but would stitch Hilton's tubular tyres for him devotedly.

He remembers how he once took her for a drink at a pub in Stratford and bought her a bottle of stout, which she had never tasted. She took a long draught straight from the bottle before declaring: "Oh, Timoshenko, how lovely, it tastes just like sperm!" Evidently, Fanny, like Tim himself, had been brought up in the bohemian wing of the party.

Compared with Hilton's exuberant ragbag of cycling lore, Matt Rendell travels light. His focus is tight but purposeful, so as to tell a larger story. A Significant Other concentrates on the role of what is known in cycle sport as the "*domestique*", literally the servant. Relations on a professional cycling squad are essentially feudal: the serf exists to serve his master, belongs to him, even. At any moment, the *domestique* may be called upon to sacrifice his strength, his own standing in the race, and even his bicycle to the ulterior needs of the team leader. His reward for this job, which automatically denies him glory, is to share in the spoils of the team's victory: by tradition and convention, the prize money is shared out equally among team-members.

Rendell elegantly elucidates the tactical technicalities of cycling's unique mixture of cooperation and competition, teamwork and individualism. Here he explains one of cycle racing's most salient facts, the effect of drafting or slipstreaming: "Diving into the comet's tail, the rider in second position has only to produce 71% of the first rider's work rate to maintain the same speed. Carried along by these two, riders three, four and the rest can keep up on just 64% of the first rider's graft."

This is a topic that could, of course, become a bit of a textbook. The beauty of Rendell's brief book is that he has secured the cooperation of a real-life *domestique*, the Colombian Victor

Hugo Peña, who was a key member of Lance Armstrong's US Postal squad on his way to a record-equalling fifth Tour win last year. Through Peña's transcribed first-person accounts of racing for Lance, Rendell places us right in the midst of the swarming bunch. It is the details that tell: who, watching the Tour on TV, thinks of the journeyman pro's daily struggle to force down bowls of pasta and rice for breakfast – the carbohydrate fuel vital for the day, when thousands of calories will be expended during hours in the saddle?

In his choice of Peña, who proves an unusually articulate subject, Rendell hit gold: Peña himself won the leader's yellow jersey after his team's performance in the team trial on stage 4. Three days later, Peña was back in 103rd place, not because he could not climb the Alpine passes as well as anyone, but because he had dedicated himself to protecting the interests of his leader, Armstrong. Rendell could not have found a more precise illustration of the pathos of the domestique's debt of duty and his sacrifice.

Saturday July 5, 2003

As the Tour de France reaches its centenary, Matt Seaton picks the best of the celebratory books

Le Tour: A History of the Tour de France by Geoffrey Wheatcroft, 392pp, Simon & Schuster, £16.99

The Yellow Jersey Companion to the Tour de France edited by Les Woodland, 412pp, Yellow Jersey, £16

The Official Tour de France Centennial 1903-2003 L'equipe, Lance Armstrong, Jean-Marie Leblanc, 360pp, Weidenfeld, £25

A Century of Cycling: The Classic Races and Legendary Champions by William Fotheringham, 176pp, Mitchell Beazley, £20

Le Tour: A Century of the Tour de France by Jeremy Whittle, 256pp, Collins, £25

Golden Stages of the Tour de France edited by Richard Allchin and Adrian Bell, 180pp, Mousehold Press, £12.95

From its birth in 1903, the Tour de France has always been a spectacle of brutal excess. Of all sporting events, it is perhaps the most Darwinian, pitching men against each other in a race that rewards, quite literally, the survival of the fittest.

Not surprisingly, then, the Tour has always aroused strong emotions. In its early days, the rivalries between riders, and between their fans, were often close to murderous. Later races may have been better regulated, yet the combat between contenders has always retained that gladiatorial quality. But how could a mere bicycle race stir such passions? What is it that drives riders to push themselves beyond endurance, to risk life and limb and to go to almost any lengths, sometimes illegal ones, in the hunt for glory?

Money is part of the answer, naturally. The commercial imperative was there at the Tour's founding moment: as is rehearsed even, to its credit, in the official centennial book, the idea of a race around all France was a promotional idea dreamed up by a struggling sports news sheet that had been launched in 1900 by two rightwing industrialists who had angrily withdrawn their advertising from the established sports newspaper, Le Vélo, because of its editor's vociferous support for the persecuted Jewish army officer Alfred Dreyfus.

The race organised by the editor of L'Auto-Vélo, Henri Desgrange, still bears his stamp. A dour former professional rider himself, Desgrange ruled the Tour in a dictatorial and semi-sadistic manner for more than 30 years, only reluctantly allowing riders such luxuries as eating en route and using bicycles with gears. What is excessive about the Tour – the extreme demands it places on the athletes, sometimes likened to running a marathon every day for three weeks – owes much to his presiding genius. This year, Les Woodland informs us, for the first time in nearly two decades, a sponsor's logo on the leader's *maillot jaune* (yellow jersey) will be replaced by his initials, "HD".

And money was the motivation, of course, for the riders in those early editions of the Tour. Mostly it was prize money, but even then, in the first golden age of cycling, the top riders – such as Maurice Garin, who won the first two races – were also supported by manufacturers. Traditionally (and this remained true until relatively recently), the peloton was peopled by young men for whom a gruelling life on the road seemed a comparatively attractive and potentially lucrative alternative to toiling down mines or in fields.

The "dull compulsion of the economic", as Marx put it, may have propelled the Tour into existence, but that does not explain why it became one of the largest sporting spectacles in the world, with an international television audience running into the hundreds of millions and which, it is estimated, draws at least 10% of France's population to its roadsides. The answer lies in that word "spectacle".

Unlike many sporting events, the Tour has a natural narrative structure. There is a beginning (the prologue time trial and then the fast, flat stages contested by sprinters); a middle (the Alps and the Pyrenees, where the real contenders assert themselves); and an end (the final showpiece race into Paris, up and down the Champs-Elysées).

At its best, "*la grande boucle*" (literally, the "big belt") is a Ulyssean epic, in which the hero of heroes emerges, through many trials of strength, courage and endurance, to win the prize and return home victorious. This is why the Tour has gathered poets, philosophers and artists among its ranks of fans: subliminally, we devotees follow the Tour as if making a pilgrimage, because its perennial drama offers us a metaphor for the human condition. It appeals to a fundamental need to believe in nobility in the face of suffering.

One should not forget that France remains, in spirit, a Catholic country – as do Spain, Italy and Belgium, the other great nations of cycling champions. As Julian Barnes noted in a brilliant essay in Something to Declare (his collection of pieces about France), the Tour has a quality of communal religious event. During one of the event's earliest doping scandals, in 1924, a disgruntled Henri Pelissier opened up his pill-box for the astonished reporter Albert Londres, and remarked: "You have no idea what the Tour de France is. It's a Calvary. But the road to the Cross had 14 stations; we have 15 [stages of the race]."

The Tour's underpinning religious theme perhaps offers an insight into why its history has been beset by such cyclical drug scandals – always soon forgiven and forgotten. The suffering of riders is so extreme that it is understandable that they should seek help; they are only human, after all, and doping is merely a venal offence: fans are always ready to offer redemption to the once-busted rider who, now "clean", wins.

Of these books, it is easy enough to pick a winner, though each deserves a coloured jersey or place on the podium for different reasons. Geoffrey Wheatcroft has the distinction of being the most natural writer of the bunch – and the only non-specialist, which, in fact, proves a strength as he brings a fresh eye to the Tour and a larger view of its cultural context. Well-read and genial, this self-confessed armchair athlete proves a surprisingly adept historian, even if one senses in the last third of the book that his decision to give a year-by-year account of every Tour since 1903 was a feat of endurance that severely taxed his enthusiasm. But like a true *touriste*, he stays the course.

Woodland, a longtime cycling journalist, has done an equally compendious job. The scores of entries in his Companion, if occasionally prosaic in content, are always entertainingly written; the elaborate cross-referencing easily carries one on a rewarding paperchase of excellent Tour trivia. Woodland is also represented as a contributor to Golden Stages, a collection in which a squad of cycling journalists recalls favourite stages of the Tour. Consisting of edited highlights, this is a budget book for the serious fan, for whom a passion for the content overcomes too much concern with style. Still, it contains one of the most iconic photographs of the Tour, not reproduced in the more lavish productions: René Vietto sitting on a dry-stone wall, his bike minus its front wheel hooked over a rock next to him, on Stage 15 of the 1934 Tour. The rookie rider Vietto had given his wheel to Antonin Magne, a former winner and the French team leader, who had broken a rim towards the end of this first stage in the Pyrenees. Vietto was soon resupplied by the service truck, and was scarcely a challenger for the *maillot jaune* in any case; yet his loyal gesture became "the sacrifice of Vietto" – "hot tears", as the original caption had it, coursed down his cheeks while he waited.

The other three centenary volumes are heavily illustrated. William Fotheringham (known to many readers of this newspaper as its cycling correspondent, and author recently of a fine biography of Tommy Simpson) provides A Century of Cycling with a "worth-reading index" far above its somewhat magazine-like combination of text and pictures. Its unique selling point is that it chooses to feature not only the Tour but also the "classics", such as the Milan-San Remo and the Paris-Roubaix, that fill professional cycling's racing calendar.

Le Tour provides minimal text, just a desultory few paragraphs for each decade, but Jeremy Whittle's captions are judicious. This book's handicap also proves its strength: because The Official Centennial publication has exclusive access to the Tour's photo archive (courtesy of L'Equipe, successor to Desgrange's L'Auto-Vélo), Le Tour has to rely on independent agency pictures. These tend to have less the flavour of pure sports photography and more of reportage; of all the books here, then, Whittle's book provides possibly the most vivid and least familiar impressions of the Tour's real character.

The Official Centennial makes the least satisfying reading, due mainly to the difficulties of rendering the often-overheated prose of the original French sports writing. But, as it is the official version, it is stunningly illustrated. It is a book to be browsed backwards, for the further back you turn, the more poignant the photographs: the early riders, wearing their spare tyres like bandoliers and with their odd caps and goggles, look like a cross between circus performers and French foreign legionnaires. In a sense, that is exactly what they were: their job was to fight and to entertain. And, of course, to suffer.

Saturday June 17, 2006

The Hour: Sporting Immortality the Hard Way by Michael Hutchinson, 288pp, Yellow Jersey Press, £10.99

"The Hour" occupies a unique place in cycle sport, perhaps a unique place in sport generally. It is, simply, the maximum distance a cyclist can ride in the course of a single hour on a velodrome track. Cycling has many races to run: the Tour de France, the world championships, the various Olympic titles – the list is endless. But, down the years, the Hour has exercised a special lure of its own, dragging the supreme riders of each era into the game of orbiting a banked 250m circuit at lung-bursting speed: Fausto Coppi, Jacques Anquetil, Francesco Moser, Eddy Merckx – virtually all the greats have at one time held the Hour record. It has a purity of purpose, offering riders a way of measuring themselves unambiguously against the all-time best. The Hour is the blue riband of cycling.

And it has an uncommon depth of human drama behind its history of record attempts. Sometimes, the Hour has been the stage for the most bitter and intense rivalries. Michael Hutchinson relates with relish the pre-first-world-war battles between Oscar Egg and Marcel Berthet, who took the mark off each other five times in the space of two years. On one occasion, Egg took to the track with a tape measure to prove that each lap was 1.7m longer than previously thought, thus adding a couple of kilometres to his 1912 record without having to remount his bike.

More recently, in the early 1990s, the cycling world was transfixed by the duel between Chris Boardman, whose career was built on the meticulous application of sports science, and Graeme Obree, a maverick Scotsman who put together his bike from, among other things, old washing machine parts. More often, though, the Hour has been a way for cycling's greatest champions to add a final polish to their *palmares*, to stake an undeniable claim to what Hutchinson rightly calls sporting immortality.

But, while this book does an admirable job of retelling the old anecdotes with a delicious sardonic wit, the real story is Hutchinson's own attempt on the Hour in 2003. It is unlikely that you will have heard of Hutchinson the cyclist, even though he has dominated the British time-trialling scene in recent years. He is a very extraordinary athlete, but – and he would be the first to admit it – the British time-trialling scene is a peculiar and obscure sporting subculture. So what kind of hubris was it that made "Hutch" think he could attack a record that is now too intimidating for even cycling's established world-beaters to attempt?

This is a question that Hutchinson frequently asks himself over the course of his torturous preparation for the event. In fact, he had very reasonable grounds for believing he could beat it. He knew that he could sustain for an hour a wattage very close to what was required. But for a successful effort, everything would have to be perfect: from the set-up of the bike to make him as aerodynamic as possible, to variables beyond his control such as the air pressure on the day. What follows is an often hilarious tale of sporting obsession bordering on the psychotic. And all in pursuit of a quest that comes to seem increasingly quixotic, as the grandeur of the ambition is gradually undermined by inevitable mishaps.

It all adds up to another episode in the venerable tradition of British sporting failure. It is perhaps a familiar theme, but Hutchinson proves as good a writer as he is rider (praise indeed) – congenial, funny and insightful. Yes, he did fall short of sporting immortality, but his book is a very fine way indeed to spend an hour, any hour.